soups
& *starters*

soups
& *starters*

SIMPLY SENSATIONAL DISHES FOR EVERY
MEAL AND ANY OCCASION

LINDA FRASER

LORENZ BOOKS

This edition first published by Lorenz Books
27 West 20th Street, New York, NY 10011

LORENZ BOOKS are available for bulk purchase for sales promotion
and for premium use. For details, write or call the sales director,
Lorenz Books, 27 West 20th Street, New York, NY 10011;
(800) 354-9657

ISBN 0-7548-0269-8

A CIP catalogue record for this book is available from the British Library

Publisher: Joanna Lorenz
Senior Cookery Editor: Linda Fraser
Designers: Tony Paine and Roy Prescott
Photographers: Steve Baxter, Karl Adamson and Amanda Heywood
Food for Photography: Wendy Lee, Jane Stevenson and Elizabeth Wolf-Cohen
Props Stylists: Blake Minton and Kirsty Rawlings
Additional recipes: Carla Capalbo and Laura Washburn

Front Cover: William Lingwood, Photographer; Helen Trent, Stylist;
Sunil Vijayakar, Home Economist

Printed in Hong Kong/China

1 3 5 7 9 10 8 6 4 2

ACKNOWLEDGEMENTS
For their assistance in the publication of this book,
the publishers wish to thank:

Kenwood Appliances plc
New Lane
Havant
Hants PO9 2NH

Magimix
115A High Street
Godalming, Surrey
GU7 1AQ

Prestige
Prestige House
22-26 High Street
Egham
Surrey
TW20 9DU

Le Creuset
The Kitchenware Merchants Ltd
4 Stephenson Close
East Portway
Andover
Hampshire SP10 3RU

🍎 The apple symbol indicates a low fat, low cholesterol recipe.

CONTENTS

STOCKS FOR SOUPS

There's no doubt that the best soups are based on homemade stock, and although stocks can be time-consuming to make, their superior flavor makes all the effort worthwhile. Stock can of course be prepared ahead, when you have the time to cook and the ingredients on hand – some stocks will keep for up to four or five days in the fridge, and for as long as six months in the freezer. There are four main types of stock: fish, vegetable, meat and poultry, and here we guide you through the techniques and processes, step-by-step. Vegetable and fish stocks are quickest to prepare as they only need simmering for about half an hour.

MAKING FISH STOCK

Fish stock is much quicker to make than meat or poultry stock. Ask your fishmonger for heads, bones and trimmings from white fish.

Makes about 4 cups

1½lb heads, bones and trimmings from
   white fish
1 onion, sliced
2 celery sticks with leaves, chopped
1 carrot, sliced
½ lemon, sliced (optional)
1 bay leaf
a few fresh parsley sprigs
6 black peppercorns
5⅓ cups water
⅔ pint dry white wine

1 Rinse the fish heads, bones and trimmings well under cold running water. Put in a stockpot with the vegetables, lemon, if using, the herbs, peppercorns, water and wine. Bring to a boil, skimming the surface frequently, then reduce the heat and simmer for 25 minutes.

2 Strain the stock without pressing down on the ingredients in the sieve. If not using immediately, leave to cool and then chill. Fish stock should be used within 2 days, or it can be frozen for up to 3 months.

MAKING VEGETABLE STOCK

Vary the ingredients for this fresh-flavored stock according to what you have to hand. Chill, covered, for up to 5 days; freeze up to 1 month.

Makes about 10 cups

2 large onions, coarsely chopped
2 leeks, sliced
3 garlic cloves, crushed with the flat
   side of a knife
3 carrots, coarsely chopped
4 celery sticks, coarsely chopped
a large strip of lemon rind
a handful of parsley stalks (about 12)
a few fresh thyme sprigs
2 bay leaves
10 cups water

1 Put the vegetables, lemon rind, herbs and water in a stockpot and bring to a boil. Skim off the foam that rises to the surface, frequently at first and then from time to time.

2 Reduce the heat and simmer, uncovered, for 30 minutes. Strain the stock and leave it to cool.

MAKING POULTRY STOCK

A good home-made poultry stock is invaluable in the kitchen. It is simple and economical to make, and can be stored in the freezer for up to six months. If poultry giblets are available, add them to the stockpot (except the livers) with the wings.

Makes about 2 quarts

2½–3lb poultry wings, backs and necks (chicken, turkey, etc)
2 onions, unpeeled and quartered
4 quarts cold water
2 carrots, roughly chopped
2 celery stalks, with leaves if possible, roughly chopped
a small handful of fresh parsley
a few fresh thyme sprigs or 1 tsp dried thyme
1 or 2 bay leaves
10 black peppercorns, lighly crushed

A FRUGAL STOCK

Stock can be made from the bones and carcasses of roasted poultry, cooked with vegetables and flavorings. Save the carcasses in a polythene bag in the freezer until you have three or four, then make stock. It may not have quite as rich a flavor as stock made from a whole bird or fresh wings, backs and necks, but it will still taste fresher and less salty than stock made from a cube.

1 Combine the poultry wings, backs and necks and the onions in a stockpot. Cook over moderate heat, stirring occasionally so they color evenly, until lightly browned.

2 Add the water and stir well to mix in the sediment on the bottom of the pot. Bring to the boil and skim off the impurities as they rise to the surface of the stock.

3 Add the remaining ingredients. Partly cover the stockpot and gently simmer the stock for 3 hours.

4 Strain the stock into a bowl and leave to cool, then refrigerate.

5 When cold, remove the layer of fat that will have set on the surface.

STOCK TIPS

If wished, use a whole bird for making stock instead of wings, backs and necks. A boiling fowl will give a wonderful flavor and provide plenty of chicken meat to use in soups and casseroles.

No salt is added to stock because as the stock reduces the flavor becomes concentrated and saltiness increases. Add salt to the dish in which the stock is used.

MAKING MEAT STOCK

The most delicious meat soups rely on a good home-made stock for success. Neither a stock cube nor a canned consommé will do if you want the best flavor. Once made, meat stock can be kept in the refrigerator for four or five days, or frozen for longer storage (up to six months).

ON THE LIGHT SIDE

For a light meat stock, use veal bones and do not roast the bones or vegetables. Put in the pot with cold water and cook as described.

Makes about 2 quarts

4lb beef bones, such as shank, knuckle, and leg, or veal or lamb bones, cut into 2½in pieces
2 onions, unpeeled, quartered
2 carrots, roughly chopped
2 celery sticks, with leaves if possible, roughly chopped
2 tomatoes, coarsely chopped
4 quarts cold water
a handful of parsley stalks
a few fresh thyme sprigs or 1 tsp dried thyme
2 bay leaves
10 black peppercorns, lightly crushed

1 Preheat the oven to 450°F. Put the bones in a roasting pan or flameproof casserole and roast, turning occasionally, for 30 minutes or until they start to brown.

2 Add the onions, carrots, celery and tomatoes and baste with the fat in the tin. Roast for a further 20-30 minutes or until the bones are well browned. Stir and baste occasionally.

3 Transfer the bones and vegetables to a stockpot. Spoon off the fat from the roasting pan or casserole.

4 Add a little of the water to the roasting pan or casserole and bring to a boil on top of the stove, stirring well to scrape up any browned bits. Pour this liquid into the stockpot.

5 Add the remaining water. Bring just to a boil, skimming frequently to remove all the foam from the surface. Add the parsley, thyme, bay leaves and peppercorns.

6 Partly cover the pot and simmer for 4–6 hours. The bones and vegetables should always be covered with liquid, so top up with boiling water from time to time if necessary.

7 Strain the stock. Skim as much fat as possible from the surface, then cool the stock and chill it; the fat will rise to the top and set in a layer that can be removed easily.

PREPARING STARTERS

Starters are usually served at the beginning of special meals, or when you are entertaining, so they need either to be easy to put together at the last minute, or able to be prepared ahead. The recipe sections include all sorts of hot and cold starters, and here we give you some special techniques: from making perfect mayonnaise and vinaigrette dressing, to preparing, cooking – and eating – a globe artichoke. You'll also discover just how easy it is to make a classic hollandaise sauce with our simple method, the secrets of cooking asparagus spears – along with tips, helpful hints and serving suggestions.

MAKING VINAIGRETTE DRESSING

A good vinaigrette can do more than dress a salad. It can also be used to baste meat, poultry, seafood or vegetables during cooking; and it can be used as a flavoring and tenderizing marinade. The basic mixture of oil, vinegar and seasoning lends itself to many variations.

The basic dressing will keep in the refrigerator, in a tightly closed container, for several weeks. Add flavorings, such as fresh herbs, just before using.

Makes just over ¾ cup
3 tbsp wine vinegar
½ cup plus 2 tbsp vegetable oil
salt and black pepper

1 Put the vinegar, salt and pepper in a bowl and whisk to dissolve the salt. Gradually add the oil, stirring with the whisk. Taste and adjust seasoning.

IDEAS FOR VINAIGRETTE

- Use a herb-flavored vinegar.
- Use lemon juice instead of vinegar.
- Use olive oil, or a mixture of vegetable and olive oils.
- Use ½ cup olive oil and 2 tbsp walnut or hazelnut oil.
- Add 1–2 tbsp Dijon mustard to the vinegar before whisking in the oil.
- Add 1 crushed garlic clove.
- Add 1–2 tbsp chopped fresh herbs (parsley, basil, chives, thyme, etc) to the vinaigrette.

MAKING MAYONNAISE

This cold emulsified sauce of oil and egg yolk has thousands of uses – as part of a dish or as an accompaniment, in sandwiches and in salad dressings. It can be varied by using different oils, vinegars and flavorings.

Makes about 1½ cups
2 egg yolks
1½ cups oil (vegetable, corn or olive)
1–2 tbsp lemon juice
1–2 tsp Dijon mustard
salt and black pepper

WATCHPOINT

Remember that foods containing raw eggs shouldn't be eaten by children, pregnant mothers, the elderly or the sick.

1 Beat the egg yolks in a bowl with a pinch of salt. Add the oil, 1–2 tsp at a time, beating constantly. After one-quarter of the oil has been added beat in 1–2 tsp of the lemon juice. Continue beating in the oil, in a thin, steady stream and as the mayonnaise thickens, add another teaspoon of lemon juice.

2 When all the oil has been beaten in, add the mustard. Taste the mayonnaise and add more lemon juice or vinegar. Season with salt and pepper. If the mayonnaise is too thick, beat in a spoonful or two of water. Home-made mayonnaise will keep, covered in the refrigerator, for up to 1 week. It should not be frozen.

MAKING SIMPLE HOLLANDAISE SAUCE

This classic of French cuisine has a reputation for being difficult to make. Harold McGee has devised a method of putting all the ingredients in the pan at once, which lowers the chance of failure. Be careful not to allow the sauce to become too hot, or it will separate. Just take it slow and steady, and whisk constantly.

Makes about 1¼ cups
3 egg yolks
1 tbsp lemon juice, plus more
   if needed
a pinch of cayenne
1 cup butter, preferably unsalted,
   cut into 1 tbsp chunks
salt and black pepper

1 Combine the egg yolks, lemon juice, cayenne, salt and pepper in a heavy saucepan. Whisk together well. Add the butter and set the pan over moderate heat. Whisk constantly so that as the butter melts it is blended into the egg yolks.

2 When all the butter has melted and has been blended into the egg yolk base, continue whisking until the sauce just thickens to a creamy consistency. Taste the sauce and add more lemon juice, salt and pepper if needed.

PREPARING ASPARAGUS

When asparagus is young and tender, you need do nothing more than trim off the ends of the stalks. However, larger spears, with stalk ends that are tough and woody, require some further preparation.

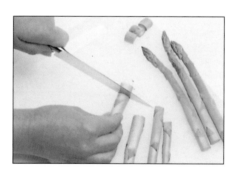

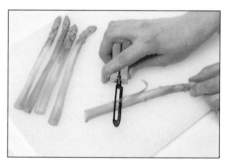

1 Cut off the tough, woody ends. Cut the spears so they are all about the same length.

2 If you like, remove the skin: lay a spear flat and hold it just below the tip. With a vegetable peeler, shave off the skin, working lengthwise down the spear to the end of the stalk. Roll the spear so you can remove the skin from all sides.

ASPARAGUS WITH HOLLANDAISE SAUCE

Prepare 1½lb asparagus. Arrange the spears on a rack in a steamer over simmering water, cover and steam for 8–12 minutes, or simmer in a large frying pan with water just to cover for 4–5 minutes, until just tender when pierced with the tip of a knife. Transfer to warmed plates and spoon over the hollandaise sauce. *Serves 4.*

UPRIGHT COOKING

Asparagus spears can be cooked loose and flat in simmering water or tied into bundles and cooked standing upright in a tall pot. With the latter method, the tips are kept above the water so they cook gently in the steam.

Preparing and Cooking Globe Artichokes

Artichokes can be served whole, with or without a stuffing, or just the meaty bottoms, or bases, may be used. Very small artichokes, 2½in or less in diameter, are often called hearts; this can be confusing, as artichoke bottoms are also sometimes called hearts. These baby artichokes are best braised whole, or halved or quartered. Be sure to rub all cut surfaces with lemon juice as you work and use a stainless steel knife, to prevent darkening and discoloration.

Artichokes with Herb Butter

Serve boiled artichokes hot with clarified butter mixed with 1–2 tbsp chopped fresh dill and parsley or other herbs.

Eating Artichokes

One by one, pull off a leaf and dip the base into the sauce. Scrape the flesh from the base of the leaf with your teeth, then discard the leaf. When you have removed all the large leaves, you will have exposed the fuzzy choke. Scrape this off and discard it. Cut the meaty bottom, or base, of the artichoke for eating with a fork.

1 **Whole artichokes**: break off the stalk close to the base. Cut off the pointed top about one-third of the way down. Snip off the pointed end of each large outside leaf using scissors. Open up the leaves and rinse thoroughly between them.

3 **To cook whole artichokes**: bring a large pot of salted water to a boil. Add the juice of 1 lemon or 3–4 tablespoons vinegar. Add the prepared artichokes and put a plate on top to keep them submerged. Cover and simmer until you can pierce the stalk end easily with a fork: 15–20 minutes for small artichokes, 25–50 minutes for large artichokes.

5 **To cook artichoke bottoms**: boil gently in salted water to cover for 15–20 minutes or until tender.

2 **Artichoke bottoms**: break off all the coarse outer leaves down to the pale inner leaves. Scrape off the fuzzy center, or "choke" (or do this after cooking) and peel away all the leaves with a stainless steel knife, leaving just the edible base or bottom.

4 Remove and drain well, upside-down. Open up the leaves so you can insert a spoon into the center and scrape out the fuzzy choke.

Ideas for Artichokes

- Serve boiled artichokes hot with hollandaise sauce.
- Serve boiled artichokes cool (not chilled) with a vinaigrette dressing or mayonnaise.
- Serve cool artichoke bottoms filled with prawn or crab mayonnaise salad.
- Boil artichoke bottoms with flavorings such as garlic, bay leaf and black peppercorns. Drain and cool, then slice and marinate in a vinaigrette dressing with chopped onion and olives.

LIGHT SOUPS

A bowl of soup makes a tasty light meal or a flavorful starter, and before a substantial main course, soups that are neither too rich, nor too chunky are ideal. There are recipes here for everyday meals, and some deliciously different tastes to try when you are entertaining, such as Red Bell Pepper Soup with Lime. Of course, the weather doesn't have to be cold for soup to be appealing, there are superb summer soups, too; choose from a creamy version of the classic Vichyssoise, a chilled avocado soup, or the spicy, yet refreshing Gazpacho.

Tomato and Basil Soup

In summer, when tomatoes are plentiful and cheap to buy, this is a lovely soup to make.

Ingredients

Serves 4

2 tbsp olive oil
1 onion, chopped
½ tsp sugar
1 carrot, finely chopped
1 potato, finely chopped
1 garlic clove, crushed
1½lb ripe tomatoes, roughly chopped
1 tsp tomato paste
1 bay leaf
1 thyme sprig
1 oregano sprig
4 basil leaves, roughly torn
1¼ cups light chicken or vegetable
   stock
2–3 pieces sun-dried tomatoes in oil
2 tbsp shredded basil leaves
salt and black pepper

1 Heat the oil in a large pan, add the onion and sprinkle with the sugar. Cook gently for 5 minutes.

2 Add the chopped carrot and potato, cover the pan and cook over a low heat for a further 10 minutes, without browning the vegetables.

3 Stir in the garlic, tomatoes, tomato paste, herbs, stock and seasoning. Cover and cook gently for 25–30 minutes, until the vegetables are tender.

4 Remove the pan from the heat and press the soup through a sieve or food mill to extract all the skins and seeds. Taste and adjust seasoning.

5 Reheat the soup gently, then ladle into four warmed soup bowls. Finely chop the sun-dried tomatoes and mix with a little oil from the jar. Add a spoonful to each serving, then scatter the shredded basil over the top.

Spiced Pumpkin Soup

INGREDIENTS

Serves 4

2 tbsp butter
1 onion, finely chopped
1 small garlic clove, crushed
1 tbsp flour
pinch of grated nutmeg
½ tsp ground cinnamon
3 cups seeded, peeled and cubed
  pumpkin
2½ cups chicken stock
⅔ cup orange juice
1 tsp brown sugar
1 tbsp vegetable oil
2 slices whole grain bread, crusts
  removed
2 tbsp sunflower seeds
salt and black pepper

1 Heat the butter in a large pan, add the onions and garlic and fry gently for 4–5 minutes, until softened.

2 Stir in the flour, spices and pumpkin, then cover and cook gently for 6 minutes, stirring occasionally.

3 Pour in the chicken stock and orange juice and add the brown sugar. Cover and bring to a boil, then reduce the heat and simmer for 20 minutes, until the pumpkin has softened.

4 Pour half of the mixture into a blender or food processor and whizz until smooth. Return the soup to the pan with the remaining chunky mixture, stirring constantly. Season well and heat through.

5 Meanwhile, make the croûtons. Heat the oil in a frying pan, cut the bread into cubes and fry gently until just beginning to brown. Add the sunflower seeds and fry for 1–2 minutes. Drain the croûtons on paper towels.

6 Serve the soup hot with a few of the croûtons scattered over the top. Serve the rest separately.

Chilled Leek and Potato Soup

This creamy, chilled soup is a version of the *vichyssoise* originally created by a French chef at the Ritz Carlton Hotel in New York to celebrate the opening of the roof gardens.

INGREDIENTS

Serves 4
2 tbsp butter
1 tbsp vegetable oil
1 small onion, chopped
3 leeks, sliced
2 potatoes, diced
2½ cups vegetable stock
1¼ cups milk
3 tbsp light cream
a little extra milk (optional)
salt and black pepper
4 tbsp natural yogurt and a few
   snipped chives, to garnish

1 Heat the butter and oil in a large pan and add the onion, leeks and potatoes. Cover and simmer for 15 minutes, stirring occasionally. Stir in the stock and milk and simmer for 10 minutes, until the potatoes are tender.

2 Ladle the vegetables and liquid into a blender or food processor in batches and purée until smooth. Return the soup to the pan, stir in the cream and season well.

3 Leave the soup to cool, and then chill for 3–4 hours, or until really cold. You may need to add a little extra milk to thin down the soup, as it will thicken slightly as it cools.

4 Serve the chilled soup in individual bowls, topped with a spoonful of natural yogurt and a sprinkling of snipped fresh chives.

Curried Parsnip Soup

The spices impart a delicious, mild curry flavor which carries an exotic breath of India.

INGREDIENTS

Serves 4
2 tbsp butter
1 garlic clove, crushed
1 onion, chopped
1 tsp ground cumin
1 tsp ground coriander
3½ cups (about 4) parsnips, sliced
2 tsp medium curry paste
2 cups chicken stock
2 cups milk
4 tbsp sour cream
squeeze of lemon juice
salt and black pepper
fresh coriander sprigs, to garnish
ready-made garlic and coriander naan
   bread, to serve

1 Heat the butter in a large pan and add the garlic and onion. Fry gently for 4–5 minutes, until lightly golden. Stir in the spices and cook for a further 1–2 minutes.

2 Add the parsnips and stir until well coated with the butter, then stir in the curry paste, followed by the stock. Cover the pan and simmer for 15 minutes, until the parsnips are tender.

3 Ladle the soup into a blender or food processor and whizz until smooth. Return to the pan and stir in the milk. Heat gently for 2–3 minutes, then add 2 tbsp of the sour cream and the lemon juice. Season well.

4 Serve in bowls topped with spoonfuls of the remaining sour cream and the fresh coriander, accompanied by the naan bread.

Spiced Carrot Soup with Yogurt

Use a good homemade stock for this soup, if possible – it adds a far greater depth of flavor than stock made from cubes.

INGREDIENTS

Serves 4

4 tbsp butter
3 leeks, sliced
1lb carrots, sliced
1 tbsp ground coriander
5 cups light chicken stock
⅔ cup strained plain yogurt
salt and black pepper
2–3 tbsp chopped fresh coriander,
   to garnish

1 Melt the butter in a large pan. Add the leeks and carrots and stir well, coating the vegetables with the butter. Cover and cook for about 10 minutes, until the vegetables are beginning to soften but not color.

2 Stir in the ground coriander and cook for about 1 minute. Pour in the stock and add seasoning to taste. Bring to a boil, cover and simmer for about 20 minutes, until the leeks and carrots are tender.

3 Leave to cool slightly, then purée the soup in a blender until smooth. Return the soup to the pan and add 2 tbsp of the yogurt, then taste the soup and adjust the seasoning. Reheat gently but do not boil.

4 Ladle the soup into bowls and put a spoonful of the remaining yogurt in the center of each. Scatter over the coriander and serve immediately.

Creamy Arugula Soup with Croûtons

Arugula, with its distinctive, peppery taste, is wonderful in this filling and satisfying soup. Serve it hot with ciabatta croûtons.

INGREDIENTS

Serves 4–6

4 tbsp butter
1 onion, chopped
3 leeks, chopped
2 potatoes, diced
3¾ cups light chicken stock
  or water
2 large handfuls arugula, roughly
  chopped
⅔ cup heavy cream
salt and black pepper
garlic-flavored ciabatta croûtons,
  to serve

1 Melt the butter in a large heavy-based pan, add the onion, leeks and potatoes and stir until the vegetables are coated in butter.

2 Cover and leave the vegetables to sweat for about 15 minutes. Pour in the stock, cover once again, then simmer for a further 20 minutes, until the vegetables are tender.

3 Press the soup through a sieve or food mill and return to the rinsed-out pan. (When puréeing the soup, don't use a blender or food processor, as these will give the soup a gluey texture.) Add the chopped arugula and cook gently for 5 minutes.

4 Stir in the cream, then season to taste and reheat gently. Ladle the soup into warmed soup bowls, then serve with a few garlic-flavored ciabatta croûtons in each.

Rich Tomato Soup

An all-time favorite – this fresh soup tastes so much nicer than the canned version. Make sure you use good-flavored, ripe tomatoes, or home-grown.

INGREDIENTS

Serves 4
2lb (about 12 medium) tomatoes
1 tbsp olive oil
1 large onion, chopped
1 garlic clove, crushed
1 potato, chopped
1 tbsp tomato paste
1 tsp sugar
salt and black pepper
4 tbsp sour cream
fresh chervil sprigs, to garnish

1 Place the tomatoes in a large heatproof bowl. Cover them with boiling water and leave to stand for about 1–2 minutes.

2 Heat the olive oil in a large pan and add the onion, garlic and potato. Fry gently for about 5 minutes, until the onion has softened.

3 Meanwhile, drain the hot water from the tomatoes, peel off the skins then halve the tomatoes and remove the cores. Chop the tomato flesh and add to the pan with the seeds, any juice and the tomato paste.

4 Pour over 1¼ cups boiling water, stir, then cover and simmer gently for about 15 minutes, until the potato has softened.

5 Purée the soup in batches in a blender or food processor until smooth. Return the soup to the pan, add the sugar, season well and heat through. Serve in bowls with a dollop of sour cream and the sprigs of fresh chervil.

French Onion Soup

INGREDIENTS

Serves 4
2 tbsp butter
1 tbsp oil
3 large onions, thinly sliced
1 tsp soft brown sugar
1 tbsp flour
2 x 10oz cans condensed beef
   consommé
2 tbsp medium sherry
2 tsp Worcestershire sauce
8 slices French bread
1 tbsp French coarse grained mustard
1 cup Gruyère cheese, grated
salt and black pepper
1 tbsp chopped fresh parsley, to garnish

1 Heat the butter and oil in a large pan and add the onions and brown sugar. Cook gently for about 20 minutes, stirring occasionally, until the onions start to turn golden brown.

2 Stir in the flour and cook for a further 2 minutes. Pour in the consommé, plus two cans of water, then add the sherry and Worcestershire sauce. Season well, cover and simmer gently for a further 25–30 minutes.

3 Preheat the broiler and, just before serving, toast the bread lightly on both sides. Spread one side of each slice with the mustard and top with the grated cheese. Grill the toasts until bubbling and golden.

4 Ladle the soup into bowls. Pop two croûtons on top of each bowl of soup and garnish with chopped fresh parsley. Serve at once.

Watercress and Orange Soup

This is a very healthy and refreshing soup, which is just as good served hot or chilled.

INGREDIENTS

Serves 4

1 large onion, chopped
1 tbsp olive oil
2 bunches or bags of watercress
grated rind and juice of 1 large orange
1 vegetable bouillon cube
⅔ cup light cream
2 tsp cornstarch
salt and black pepper
a little thick cream or yogurt, to garnish
4 orange wedges, to serve

1 Soften the onion in the oil in a large pan. Trim any big stems off the watercress, then add to the pan of onion without chopping. Cover the pan and cook the watercress for about 5 minutes until softened.

2 Add the orange rind and juice, and the bouillon cube dissolved in 2½ cups water. Bring to a boil, cover and simmer for 10–15 minutes.

3 Blend or process the soup thoroughly, and sieve if you like. Add the cream blended with the cornstarch, and seasoning to taste.

4 Bring the soup gently back to a boil, stirring until just slightly thickened. Check the seasoning and serve the soup with a swirl of cream or yogurt, and a wedge of orange to squeeze in at the last moment.

———— COOK'S TIP ————

Wash the watercress only if really necessary, it is often very clean.

Mushroom and Herb Soup

Although you can make mushroom soup with a nice smooth texture, it is more time consuming and you waste a lot of mushrooms – so enjoy the slightly nutty consistency instead!

INGREDIENTS

Serves 4

2oz hickory smoked bacon
1 white onion, chopped
1 tbsp sunflower oil
12oz flat cap field mushrooms or a mixture of wild and brown mushrooms
2½ cups good meat stock
2 tbsp sweet sherry
2 tbsp chopped, mixed fresh herbs, such as sage, rosemary, thyme or marjoram, or 2 tsp dried
salt and black pepper
4 tbsp thick Greek-style yogurt or crème fraîche and a few sprigs of marjoram or sage, to garnish

1 Coarsely chop the bacon and place in a large saucepan. Cook gently until all the fat comes out of the bacon.

2 Add the onion and soften, adding oil if necessary. Wipe the mushrooms clean, coarsely chop and add to the pan. Cover and sweat until they have completely softened and their liquid has run out.

3 Add the stock, sherry, herbs and seasoning, cover and simmer for 10–12 minutes. Blend or process the soup until smooth, but don't worry if you still have a slightly textured result.

4 Check the seasoning and heat through. Serve with a dollop of yogurt or crème fraîche and a herb sprig in each bowl.

Carrot and Coriander Soup

Carrot soup is best made with young carrots when they are at their sweetest and tastiest. With older carrots you will have to use more to get the full flavor. This soup freezes well.

INGREDIENTS

Serves 5–6
1 onion, chopped
1 tbsp sunflower oil
1½lb carrots, chopped
3¾ cups chicken stock
few sprigs coriander, or 1 tsp dried
1 tsp lemon rind
2 tbsp lemon juice
salt and black pepper
chopped fresh parsley or coriander, to
    garnish

1 Soften the onion in the oil in a large pan. Add the chopped carrots, the stock, coriander, lemon rind and juice and seasoning to taste.

2 Bring to a boil, cover and simmer for 15–20 minutes, occasionally checking that there is sufficient liquid. When the carrots are really tender, blend or process and return to the pan, then check the seasoning.

3 Heat through again and sprinkle with chopped parsley or coriander before serving.

Shrimp and Corn Chowder

This soup is perfect for informal entertaining as it is quite special but not too extravagant.

INGREDIENTS

Serves 4
1 tbsp butter
1 onion, chopped
11oz can corn
2 tbsp lemon juice
1¼ cups fish or vegetable stock
1 cup cooked, peeled shrimp
1¼ cups milk
1–2 tbsp cream or yogurt
salt and black pepper
4 large shrimp in their shells and a few
    sprigs parsley or dill, to garnish

1 Heat the butter in a pan and cook the onions until translucent. Add half the corn and all its liquid, the lemon juice, stock and half the shrimp.

2 Cover and simmer the soup for about 15 minutes, then blend or process the soup until quite smooth.

3 Return the soup to the pan and add the milk, the rest of the shrimp, chopped, and the corn, the cream or yogurt and seasoning to taste. Cook gently for 5 minutes, or until reduced sufficiently.

4 Serve each portion garnished with a whole shrimp and a herb sprig.

Chilled Avocado Soup

INGREDIENTS

Serves 4

2 large or 3 medium ripe avocados
1 tbsp fresh lemon juice
¼ cucumber, peeled and coarsely
   chopped
2 tbsp dry sherry
4 scallions, roughly chopped
2 cups chicken stock
a few drops of Tabasco sauce (optional)
salt
natural yogurt or sour cream,
   to serve

1 Halve the avocados, remove the pits, and peel. Roughly chop the flesh and place in a food processor or blender. Add the lemon juice and process until very smooth.

2 Add the cucumber, sherry and most of the chopped scallions. Process again until very smooth.

3 Transfer the avocado mixture to a large bowl, add the chicken stock and whisk until well blended. Season the soup with salt to taste and Tabasco sauce, if desired. Cover the bowl with plastic wrap and chill well.

4 To serve, pour the soup into individual bowls. Swirl a spoonful of yogurt or sour cream in the center of each bowl. Sprinkle with the reserved scallions.

Green Pea and Mint Soup

This soup is equally delicious cold. Instead of reheating it after purée-ing, leave it to cool and then chill lightly in the fridge. Stir in the swirl of cream just before serving.

INGREDIENTS

Serves 4

4 tbsp butter
4 scallions, chopped
1lb fresh or frozen peas
2½ cups chicken or
    vegetable stock
2 large mint sprigs
2½ cups milk
pinch of sugar (optional)
salt and black pepper
light cream, to serve
small mint sprigs, to garnish

1 Heat the butter in a large saucepan, add the scallions, and cook gently for a few minutes until softened but not colored.

2 Stir the peas into the pan, add the stock and mint and bring to the boil. Cover and simmer very gently for about 30 minutes for fresh peas or 15 minutes if you are using frozen peas, until the peas are very tender. Remove about 45ml/3 tbsp of the peas using a slotted spoon, and reserve for the garnish.

----- FREEZER NOTE -----

The soup can be frozen for up to two months after step 2. Allow it to thaw in the fridge before puréeing and reheating.

3 Pour the soup into a food processor or blender, add the milk and purée until smooth. Then return the soup to the pan and reheat gently. Season to taste, adding a pinch of sugar, if liked.

4 Pour the soup into bowls. Swirl a little cream into each, then garnish with mint and the reserved peas.

Beet and Apricot Swirl

This soup is most attractive if you swirl together the two colored mixtures, but if you prefer they can be mixed together to save on time and dishes.

Ingredients 🍎

Serves 4
4 large cooked beets, coarsely chopped
1 small onion, coarsely chopped
2½ cups chicken stock
1 cup dried apricots
1 cup orange juice
salt and black pepper

1 Place the beets and half the onion in a pan with the stock. Bring to a boil, then reduce the heat, cover, and simmer for about 10 minutes. Purée in a food processor or blender.

2 Place the rest of the onion in a pan with the apricots and orange juice, cover, and simmer gently for about 15 minutes, until tender. Purée in a food processor or blender.

3 Return the two mixtures to the saucepans and reheat. Season to taste with salt and pepper, then swirl them together in individual soup bowls for a marbled effect.

— Cook's Tip —

The apricot mixture should be the same consistency as the beet mixture – if it is too thick, then add a little more orange juice.

Red Bell Pepper Soup with Lime

The beautiful rich red color of this soup makes it a very attractive appetizer or light lunch. For a special dinner, toast some tiny croûtons and serve sprinkled into the soup.

INGREDIENTS 🍎

Serves 4–6

4 red bell peppers, seeded and chopped
1 large onion, chopped
1 tsp olive oil
1 garlic clove, crushed
1 small red chili, sliced
3 tbsp tomato paste
3¾ cups chicken stock
finely grated rind and juice of 1 lime
salt and black pepper
shreds of lime rind, to garnish

1 Cook the onion and bell peppers gently in the oil in a covered saucepan for about 5 minutes, shaking the pan occasionally, until softened.

2 Stir in the garlic, then add the chili with the tomato paste. Stir in half the stock, then bring to a boil. Cover the pan and simmer for 10 minutes.

3 Cool slightly, then purée in a food processor or blender. Return to the pan, then add the remaining stock, the lime rind and juice, and seasoning.

4 Bring the soup back to a boil, then serve at once with a few strips of lime rind, scattered into each bowl.

— COOK'S TIP —

Yellow or orange bell peppers could be substituted for the red peppers. And, if you don't have a fresh chili, add a drop or two of Tabasco sauce to the soup instead.

Pasta and Tomato Soup

Children will love this soup –
especially if you use fancy shapes of
pasta such as alphabet or
animal shapes.

INGREDIENTS ●

Serves 4

1½lb ripe plum tomatoes
1 medium onion, quartered
1 celery stalk
1 garlic clove
1 tbsp olive oil
1⅞ cups chicken stock
2 tbsp tomato paste
½ cup small pasta shapes
salt and black pepper
fresh coriander or parsley, to garnish

1 Place the tomatoes, onion, celery,
and garlic in a pan with the oil.
Cover and cook over low heat for
40–45 minutes, shaking the pan
occasionally, until very soft.

2 Spoon the vegetables into a food
processor or blender and process
until smooth. Press through a strainer,
then return to the pan.

3 Stir in the stock and tomato paste
and bring to a boil. Add the pasta
and simmer gently for about 8 minutes,
or until the pasta is tender. Add salt and
pepper to taste, then sprinkle with
coriander or parsley and serve hot.

COOK'S TIP

If fresh plum tomatoes are not available,
then use other flavorful, red, ripe tomatoes, or substitute canned tomatoes.

Mushroom, Celery, and Garlic Soup

INGREDIENTS ●

Serves 4

3 cups chopped mushrooms
4 celery stalks, chopped
3 garlic cloves
3 tbsp dry sherry or white wine
3⅔ cups chicken stock
2 tbsp Worcestershire sauce
1 tsp ground nutmeg
salt and black pepper
celery leaves, to garnish

COOK'S TIP

To make this soup suitable for vegetarians,
use vegetable stock in place of the chicken
stock.

1 Place the mushrooms, celery, and
garlic in a pan and stir in the sherry
or wine. Cover and cook over low
heat for 30–40 minutes, until tender.

2 Add half the stock and purée in a
food processor or blender until
smooth. Return to the pan and add the
remaining stock, the Worcestershire
sauce, and nutmeg.

3 Bring to a boil, season, and serve
hot, garnished with celery leaves.

Cauliflower and Walnut Cream

Even though there's no cream added to this soup, the cauliflower gives it a delicious, rich, creamy texture.

INGREDIENTS

Serves 4

1 medium cauliflower
1 medium onion, coarsely chopped
1⅞ cups chicken or vegetable
   stock
1⅞ cups skim milk
3 tbsp walnut pieces
salt and black pepper
paprika and chopped walnuts,
   to garnish

1 Trim the cauliflower of outer leaves and break into small florets. Place the cauliflower, onion, and stock in a large saucepan.

2 Bring to a boil, cover, and simmer for about 15 minutes, or until soft. Add the milk and walnuts, then purée in a food processor until smooth.

3 Season the soup to taste, then bring to a boil. Serve sprinkled with paprika and chopped walnuts.

VARIATION

To make Cauliflower and Almond Cream, use 3 tbsp ground almonds in place of the walnuts and add to the soup at the end of step 2.

Curried Carrot and Apple Soup

INGREDIENTS

Serves 4

2 tsp sunflower oil
1 tbsp mild curry powder
1¼lb carrots, chopped
1 large onion, chopped
1 tart baking apple, chopped
3⅔ cups chicken stock
salt and black pepper
plain low fat yogurt and carrot curls,
   to garnish

COOK'S TIP

Choose an acidic apple that will soften and fluff up as it cooks. Chop it into fairly small pieces before adding to the pan.

1 Heat the oil and gently fry the curry powder for 2–3 minutes.

2 Add the carrots, onion, and apple, stir well, then cover the pan.

3 Cook over very low heat for about 15 minutes, shaking the pan occasionally until softened. Spoon the vegetable mixture into a food processor or blender, then add half the stock and process until smooth.

4 Return to the pan and pour in the remaining stock. Bring the soup to a boil and adjust the seasoning before serving in bowls, garnished with a swirl of yogurt and a few curls of carrot.

Gazpacho

INGREDIENTS

Serves 4

½ cucumber, coarsely chopped
½ green bell pepper, seeded and
   coarsely chopped
½ red bell pepper, seeded and coarsely
   chopped
1 large tomato, coarsely chopped
2 scallions, chopped
Tabasco sauce (optional)
3 tbsp chopped fresh parsley or
   coriander, to garnish
croûtons, to serve

For the soup base

1lb ripe tomatoes, peeled, seeded
   and chopped
1 tbsp tomato catsup
2 tbsp tomato paste
¼ tsp sugar
salt and black pepper
3 tbsp sherry vinegar
¾ cup olive oil
1½ cups tomato juice

2 Add the catsup, tomato paste, sugar, salt, pepper, vinegar and oil and pulse on and off three or four times, just to blend. Transfer to a large bowl and stir in the tomato juice.

3 Place the cucumber and green and red peppers in the food processor or blender and pulse on and off until finely chopped; do not overmix.

4 Reserve about 2 tbsp of the chopped vegetables for garnishing; stir the remainder into the soup. Taste for seasoning. Mix in the chopped tomato, scallions and a dash of Tabasco sauce, if desired. Chill well.

5 To serve, ladle into bowls and sprinkle with the reserved chopped vegetables, chopped fresh parsley or coriander and the croûtons.

1 First make the soup base. Put the tomatoes in a food processor or blender and pulse on and off until just smooth, scraping the sides of the container occasionally.

COOK'S TIP

Use extra virgin olive oil in this soup for the very best flavor.

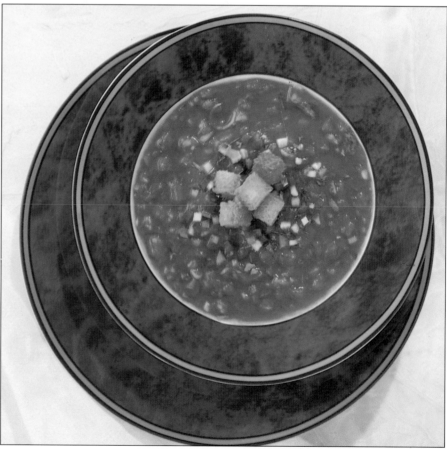

Thai-style Corn Soup

This is a very quick and easy soup, made in minutes. If you are using frozen shrimp, then defrost them first before adding to the soup.

INGREDIENTS 🍎

Serves 4

½ tsp sesame or sunflower oil
2 scallions, thinly sliced
1 garlic clove, crushed
2½ cups chicken broth
15oz can cream-style corn
1¼ cups cooked, peeled
  shrimp
1 tsp green chili paste or chili sauce
  (optional)
salt and black pepper
fresh coriander leaves, to garnish

1 Heat the oil in a large heavy-based saucepan and sauté the scallions and garlic over medium heat for 1 minute, until softened, but not browned.

2 Stir in the chicken broth, cream-style corn, shrimp, and chili paste or sauce, if using.

3 Bring the soup to a boil, stirring occasionally. Season to taste, then serve at once, sprinkled with fresh coriander leaves to garnish.

COOK'S TIP

If cream-style corn is not available, use ordinary canned corn, puréed in a food processor for a few seconds, until creamy yet with some texture left.

VARIATION

To make Thai-style Crab and Corn Soup, use canned or freshly cooked crab in place of all or some of the shrimp.

SUBSTANTIAL SOUPS

Soups are richly warming, perfect for the starving hordes on a winter's day, and, served with crusty bread, pesto-topped toasts, or crunchy croûtons, they make a filling lunch or supper. Some of the tastiest soups are traditional recipes: try Chicken and Leek Soup, or Scotch Broth from Scotland, Italian Minestrone, or thick and delicious Split Pea and Bacon Soup. Or, for a special occasion, fish or shellfish soups are also excellent – choose Mussel Bisque for an informal supper with friends, or go for a tasty bowl of Corn and Crab Chowder.

Jerusalem Artichoke Soup

Topped with saffron cream, this
soup is wonderful on a chilly day.

INGREDIENTS

Serves 4
4 tbsp butter
1 onion, chopped
1lb Jerusalem artichokes, peeled and
 cut into chunks
3¾ cups chicken stock
⅔ cup milk
⅔ cup heavy cream
good pinch of saffron powder
salt and black pepper
snipped fresh chives, to garnish

1 Melt the butter in a large heavy-
based pan and cook the onion for
5–8 minutes, until soft but not
browned, stirring occasionally.

2 Add the artichokes to the pan and
stir until coated in the butter.
Cover and cook gently for 10–15 minutes; do not allow the artichokes to
brown. Pour in the stock and milk,
then cover and simmer for 15 minutes.
Cool slightly, then process in a blender
or food processor until smooth.

3 Strain the soup back into the pan.
Add half the cream, season to taste,
and reheat gently. Lightly whip the
remaining cream and saffron powder.
Ladle the soup into warmed soup bowls
and put a spoonful of saffron cream in
the center of each. Scatter over the
snipped chives and serve at once.

Broccoli and Stilton Soup

A really easy, but rich, soup –
choose something simple to
follow, such as plainly roasted
or broiled meat, poultry or fish.

INGREDIENTS

Serves 4
12oz broccoli
2 tbsp butter
1 onion, chopped
1 leek, white part only, chopped
1 small potato, cut into chunks
2½ cups hot chicken
 stock
1¼ cups milk
3 tbsp heavy cream
4oz Stilton cheese, rind removed,
 crumbled
salt and black pepper

1 Break the broccoli into florets,
discarding tough stems. Set aside
two small florets for the garnish.

2 Melt the butter in a large pan and
cook the onion and leek until soft
but not colored. Add the broccoli and
potato, then pour in the stock. Cover
and simmer for 15–20 minutes, until
the vegetables are tender.

3 Cool slightly, then purée in a
blender or food processor. Strain
through a sieve back into the pan.

4 Add the milk, cream and seasoning
to the pan and reheat gently. At
the last minute add the cheese, stirring
until it just melts. Do not boil.

5 Meanwhile, blanch the reserved
broccoli florets and cut them
vertically into thin slices. Ladle the
soup into warmed bowls and garnish
with the broccoli florets and a generous
grinding of black pepper.

Salmon Chowder

INGREDIENTS

Serves 4

2 tbsp butter or margarine
1 onion, finely chopped
1 leek, finely chopped
1 fennel bulb, finely chopped
2 tbsp flour
5 cups fish stock
2 medium potatoes, cut into
　½in cubes
1lb boneless, skinless salmon, cut into
　¾in cubes
¾ cup milk
½ cup light cream
2 tbsp chopped fresh dill
salt and black pepper

1 Melt the butter or margarine in a large saucepan. Add the onion, leek and fennel and cook over a medium heat for 5–8 minutes, until softened, stirring occasionally.

2 Stir in the flour. Reduce the heat to low and cook, stirring occasionally, for a further 3 minutes.

3 Add the stock and potatoes and season with salt and pepper. Bring to a boil, then reduce the heat, cover, and simmer for about 20 minutes, until the potatoes are tender.

4 Add the salmon cubes and simmer for 3–5 minutes, until just cooked.

5 Stir in the milk, cream and dill and cook until just warmed through; do not boil. Taste and adjust the seasoning, if necessary, then serve.

Leek and Potato Soup

The chopped vegetables in this recipe produce a really chunky soup. If you prefer a smooth texture, press the mixture through a strainer or purée it in a food mill.

INGREDIENTS

Serves 4
4 tbsp butter
2 leeks, chopped
1 small onion, finely chopped
12oz potatoes, chopped
3¾ cups chicken or vegetable stock
salt and black pepper

1 Heat 2 tbsp of the butter in a large saucepan, add the leeks and onions and cook gently, stirring occasionally, for about 7 minutes, until softened but not browned.

COOK'S TIP

Don't use a food processor to purée this soup as it can give the potatoes a gluey consistency.

2 Add the potatoes to the pan and cook, stirring occasionally, for 2–3 minutes, then add the stock and bring to a boil. Cover the pan and simmer gently for 30–35 minutes, until the vegetables are very tender.

3 Adjust the seasoning, remove the pan from the heat and stir in the remaining butter in small pieces. Serve hot with crusty bread.

Chicken Broth with Cheese Toasts

INGREDIENTS

Serves 4

1 roasted chicken carcass
1 onion, quartered
2 celery stalks, finely chopped
1 garlic clove, crushed
few sprigs parsley
2 bay leaves
8oz can chopped tomatoes
14oz can chick-peas
2–3 tbsp leftover vegetables, chopped,
    or 1 large carrot, finely chopped
1 tbsp chopped fresh parsley
2 slices toast
¼ cup grated cheese
salt and black pepper

1 Pick off any little bits of meat from the carcass, especially from the underside where there is often some very tasty dark meat. Put aside.

2 Place the carcass, broken in half, in a large pan with the onion, half the celery, the garlic, herbs and sufficient water to cover. Cover the pan, bring to a boil and simmer for about 30 minutes, or until you are left with about 1¼ cups of liquid.

3 Strain the stock and return to the pan. Add the chicken meat, the remaining celery, the tomatoes, chickpeas (and their liquid), vegetables and parsley. Season to taste and simmer for another 7–10 minutes.

4 Meanwhile, sprinkle the toast with the cheese and grill until bubbling. Cut the toast into fingers or quarters and serve with, or floating on top of, the finished soup.

Bread and Cheese Soup

INGREDIENTS

Serves 4

4oz strong-flavored or blue cheese, or
    6oz mild cheese
2¼ cups skim milk
few pinches ground mace
4–6 slices stale bread
2 tbsp olive oil
1 large garlic clove, crushed
salt and black pepper
1 tbsp snipped chives, to garnish

1 Remove any rinds from the cheese and grate into a heavy-based, preferably non-stick pan. Add the milk and heat through very slowly, stirring frequently to make sure it does not stick and burn.

3 Mix the oil with the garlic and brush over the remaining bread. Toast until crisp, then cut into triangles or fingers. Sprinkle the soup with chives and serve with the toast.

2 When all the cheese has melted, add the mace, seasoning, and one piece of crustless bread. Cook over a very gentle heat until the bread has softened and slightly thickened the soup.

COOK'S TIP

Don't mix blue cheeses with other kinds of cheese in this soup.

Split Pea and Zucchini Soup

Rich and satisfying, this tasty and nutritious soup will warm you on a chilly winter's day.

INGREDIENTS 🍎

Serves 4
1⅞ cups yellow split peas
1 medium onion, finely chopped
1 tsp sunflower oil
2 medium zucchini, finely diced
3¾ cups chicken stock
½ tsp ground turmeric
salt and black pepper

1 Place the split peas in a bowl, cover with cold water, and leave to soak for several hours or overnight. Drain, rinse in cold water, and drain again.

2 Cook the onion in the oil in a covered pan, shaking occasionally, until soft. Reserve a handful of diced zucchini and add the rest to the pan. Cook, stirring, for 2–3 minutes.

3 Add the stock and turmeric to the pan and bring to a boil. Reduce the heat, then cover and simmer for 30–40 minutes, or until the split peas are tender. Adjust the seasoning.

4 When the soup is almost ready, bring a large saucepan of water to a boil, add the reserved diced zucchini, and cook for 1 minute, then drain and add to the soup before serving hot with warm crusty bread.

COOK'S TIP

For a quicker alternative, use split red lentils for this soup – they need no pre-soaking and cook very quickly. Adjust the amount of stock, if necessary.

VARIATION

To add a little extra color and flavor, stir in some peeled and seeded strips of fresh ripe red tomatoes.

Pasta and Bean Soup

Serve this hearty main-meal soup with tasty, pesto-topped French bread croûtons.

INGREDIENTS

Serves 4

⅔ cup dry beans (a mixture of red kidney and haricot beans), soaked in cold water overnight
1 tbsp oil
1 onion, chopped
2 celery stalks, thinly sliced
2–3 garlic cloves, crushed
2 leeks, thinly sliced
1 vegetable bouillon cube
14oz can or jar of pimientos
3--4 tbsp tomato paste
4oz pasta shapes
4 pieces French bread
1 tbsp pesto sauce
1 cup baby corn, halved
2oz each broccoli and cauliflower florets
few drops of Tabasco sauce, to taste
salt and black pepper

1 Drain the beans and place in a large pan with 5 cups water. Bring to a boil and simmer for about 1 hour, or until nearly tender.

2 When the beans are almost ready, heat the oil in a large pan and fry the vegetables for 2 minutes. Add the bouillon cube and the beans with about 2 cups of their liquid. Cover and simmer for 10 minutes.

3 Meanwhile, purée the pimientos with a little of their liquid and add to the pan. Stir in the tomato paste and pasta and cook for 15 minutes. Preheat the oven to 400°F.

4 Meanwhile, make the pesto croûtons; spread the French bread with the pesto sauce and bake for 10 minutes, or until crispy.

5 When the pasta is just cooked, add the corn, broccoli and cauliflower florets, Tabasco sauce and seasoning to taste. Heat through for 2–3 minutes and serve at once with the pesto croûtons.

Country Vegetable Soup

To ring the changes, vary the vegetables according to what is in season.

INGREDIENTS

Serves 4
4 tbsp butter
1 onion, chopped
2 leeks, sliced
2 celery stalks, sliced
2 carrots, sliced
2 small turnips, chopped
4 ripe tomatoes, skinned and chopped
4 cups chicken, veal or vegetable stock
bouquet garni
4oz green beans, chopped
salt and black pepper
chopped herbs such as tarragon,
   thyme, chives and parsley, to garnish

1 Heat the butter in a large saucepan, add the onion and leeks and cook gently until soft but not colored.

2 Add the celery, carrots and turnips and cook for 3–4 minutes, stirring occasionally. Stir in the tomatoes and stock, add the bouquet garni and simmer for about 20 minutes.

3 Add the beans to the soup and cook until all the vegetables are tender. Season to taste and serve garnished with chopped herbs.

Split Pea and Bacon Soup

Another name for this old-fashioned British soup is 'London Particular', from the dense fogs for which the city used to be notorious. The fogs in turn were named 'pea-soupers'.

INGREDIENTS

Serves 4
1 tbsp butter
4oz smoked bacon, chopped
1 large onion, chopped
1 carrot, chopped
1 celery stick, chopped
scant ½ cup split peas
5 cups chicken stock
salt and black pepper
2 thick slices firm bread, buttered and
   without crusts
2 slices bacon

1 Heat the butter in a saucepan, add the smoked bacon and cook until the fat runs. Stir in the onion, carrot and celery and cook for 2–3 minutes.

2 Add the split peas followed by the chicken stock. Bring to a boil, stirring occasionally, then cover the saucepan and simmer for 45–60 minutes, until the split peas are tender.

3 Meanwhile, preheat the oven to 350°F and bake the bread for about 20 minutes, until crisp and brown, then cut into cubes.

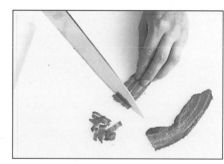

4 Broil the bacon slices until very crisp, then chop finely.

5 When the soup is ready, season to taste and serve hot with chopped bacon and croûtons scattered on each portion.

Minestrone with Pesto Toasts

This Italian mixed vegetable soup comes originally from Genoa, but the vegetables vary from region to region. This is also a great way to use up left-over vegetables.

INGREDIENTS

Serves 4

2 tbsp olive oil
2 garlic cloves, crushed
1 onion, halved and sliced
2 cups diced lean bacon
2 small zucchini, quartered
  and sliced
½ cup green beans, chopped
2 small carrots, diced
2 celery stalks, finely chopped
bouquet garni
½ cup short cut macaroni
½ cup frozen peas
7oz can red kidney beans, drained
  and rinsed
1 cup shredded green cabbage
4 tomatoes, peeled and seeded
salt and black pepper

For the toasts
8 slices French bread
1 tbsp ready-made pesto sauce
1 tbsp grated Parmesan cheese

1 Heat the oil in a large pan and gently fry the garlic and onion for 5 minutes, until just softened. Add the bacon, zucchini, green beans, carrots and celery to the pan and stir-fry for a further 3 minutes.

2 Pour 5 cups cold water over the vegetables and add the bouquet garni. Cover the pan and simmer for about 25 minutes.

3 Add the macaroni, peas and kidney beans and cook for 8 minutes. Then add the cabbage and tomatoes and cook for a further 5 minutes.

4 Meanwhile, spread the bread slices with the pesto, sprinkle a little Parmesan over each one and brown lightly under a hot broiler.

5 Remove the bouquet garni, season the soup and serve with the toasts.

COOK'S TIP

If you like, to appeal to children, you could replace the macaroni with colored pasta shapes such as shells, twists or bows.

Mulligatawny

Mulligatawny (which means 'pepper water') was introduced into England in the late eighteenth century by members of the Army and colonial service returning home from India.

INGREDIENTS

Serves 4

4 tbsp butter or oil
2 large chicken joints, about
   12oz each
1 onion, chopped
1 carrot, chopped
1 small rutabaga, chopped
about 1 tbsp curry powder,
   to taste
4 cloves
6 black peppercorns, lightly crushed
¼ cup lentils
3¾ cups chicken stock
¼ cup golden raisins
salt and black pepper

2 Add the onion, carrot and rutabaga to the pan and cook, stirring occasionally, until softened and very lightly colored. Stir in the curry powder, cloves and peppercorns and cook for 1–2 minutes, then add the lentils.

3 Pour the stock into the pan, bring to a boil, then add the golden raisins and chicken and any juices from the plate. Cover the pan and simmer gently for about 1¼ hours.

4 Remove the chicken from the pan and discard the skin and bones. Chop the flesh, return to the soup and reheat. Check the seasoning before serving the soup piping hot.

1 Melt the butter or heat the oil in a large saucepan, then brown the chicken over a high heat. Transfer the chicken to a plate.

COOK'S TIP

Choose red split lentils for the best color, although either green or brown lentils could also be used.

Chicken and Leek Soup

This traditional soup recipe – it is known from as long ago as 1598 – originally included beef as well as chicken. In the past it would have been made from an old cock bird; today we use chicken pieces.

INGREDIENTS

Serves 4–6
2 chicken portions, about 10oz each
5 cups chicken stock
bouquet garni
4 leeks
8–12 pitted prunes, soaked
salt and black pepper
soft buttered rolls, to serve

1 Gently cook the chicken, stock and bouquet garni for 40 minutes.

2 Cut the white part of the leeks into 1in slices and thinly slice a little of the green part.

3 Add the white part of the leeks and the prunes to the saucepan and cook gently for 20 minutes, then add the green part of the leeks and cook for a further 10–15 minutes.

4 Discard the bouquet garni. Remove the chicken from the pan, discard the skin and bones and chop the flesh. Return the chicken to the pan and season the soup. Heat the soup through, then serve hot with soft buttered rolls.

Scotch Broth

Sustaining and warming, Scotch Broth is custom-made for chilly Scottish weather, and makes a delicious winter soup anywhere.

INGREDIENTS

Serves 6–8
2lb lean neck of lamb, cut into large, even-sized chunks
7½ cups water
1 large onion, chopped
¼ cup pearl barley
bouquet garni
1 large carrot, chopped
1 turnip, chopped
3 leeks, chopped
½ small white cabbage, shredded
salt and black pepper
chopped parsley, to garnish

1 Put the lamb and water into a large saucepan and bring to a boil. Skim off the scum, then stir in the onion, barley and bouquet garni.

2 Bring the soup back to a boil, then partly cover the saucepan and simmer gently for 1 hour. Add the remaining vegetables and the seasoning to the pan. Bring to a boil, partly cover again and simmer for about 35 minutes until the vegetables are tender.

3 Remove surplus fat from the top of the soup, then serve hot, sprinkled with chopped parsley.

Thai Chicken Soup

INGREDIENTS

Serves 4

1 tbsp vegetable oil
1 garlic clove, finely chopped
2 x 6oz boned chicken breasts, skinned and chopped
½ tsp ground turmeric
¼ tsp hot chili powder
3oz creamed coconut
3¾ cups hot chicken stock
2 tbsp lemon or lime juice
2 tbsp chunky peanut butter
1 cup thread egg noodles, broken into small pieces
1 tbsp finely chopped scallions
1 tbsp chopped fresh coriander
salt and black pepper
2 tbsp shredded coconut and ½ fresh red chili, seeded and finely chopped, to garnish

1 Heat the oil in a large pan and fry the garlic for 1 minute until lightly golden. Add the chicken and spices and stir-fry for a further 3–4 minutes.

2 Crumble the creamed coconut into the hot chicken stock and stir until dissolved. Pour on to the chicken and add the lemon juice, peanut butter and egg noodles.

3 Cover and simmer for about 15 minutes. Add the scallions and fresh coriander, then season well and cook for a further 5 minutes.

4 Meanwhile, place the coconut and chili in a small frying pan and heat for 2–3 minutes, stirring frequently, until the coconut is lightly browned.

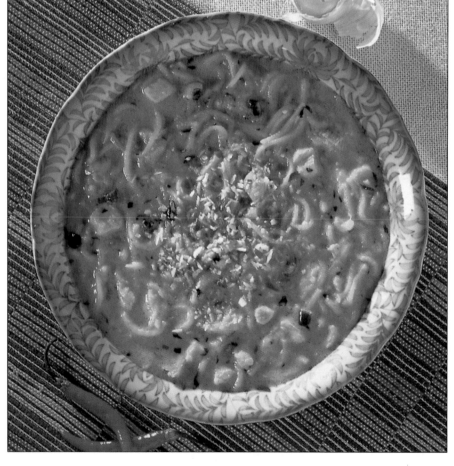

5 Serve the soup in bowls sprinkled with the fried coconut and chili.

Mussel Bisque

Served hot, this makes a delicious and very filling soup, perfect for a light, lunch-time meal. It is also excellent cold.

INGREDIENTS

Serves 6

1½lb fresh mussels in their shells
⅔ cup dry white wine or cider
2 tbsp butter
1 small red onion, chopped
1 small leek, thinly sliced
1 carrot, finely diced
2 tomatoes, skinned, seeded
  and chopped
2 garlic cloves, crushed
1 tbsp chopped fresh parsley
1 tbsp chopped fresh basil
1 celery stalk, finely sliced
½ red bell pepper, seeded and chopped
1 cup whipping cream
salt and black pepper

1 Scrub the mussels and pull off the beards. Discard any broken ones, or any that don't close when tapped. Place them in a large pan with half the wine and ⅔ cup water.

2 Cover and cook the mussels over a high heat until they open. (Discard any which don't open.) Transfer the mussels with a draining spoon to another dish and leave until cool enough to handle. Remove the mussels from their shells; leaving a few in their shells to garnish, if you like.

3 Strain the stock through a piece of cheesecloth or a fine cloth to get rid of any grit. Heat the butter in the same large pan and cook the onion, leek, carrot, tomatoes and garlic over a high heat for 2–3 minutes.

4 Reduce the heat and cook for a further 2–3 minutes, then add the cooking liquid, 1¼ cups water and the herbs and simmer for a further 10 minutes. Add the mussels, celery, pepper, cream, and seasoning. Serve hot.

Tomato and Blue Cheese Soup

INGREDIENTS

Serves 4

3lb ripe tomatoes, peeled, quartered, and seeded
2 garlic cloves, finely chopped
2 tbsp vegetable oil
1 leek, chopped
1 carrot, chopped
4 cups unsalted chicken stock
4oz blue cheese, cut into smallish pieces
3 tbsp light cream
a few fresh basil leaves, plus extra for garnishing
6oz bacon, cooked and crumbled
salt and black pepper

1 Preheat the oven to 400°F. Spread the tomatoes in a shallow baking dish with the garlic.

2 Add seasoning to taste and bake for about 35 minutes.

3 Heat the oil in a large saucepan. Add the leek and carrot and season lightly with salt and pepper. Cook over a low heat for 10 minutes, stirring occasionally, until softened.

4 Stir in the stock and tomatoes. Bring to a boil, then lower the heat, cover and simmer for 20 minutes.

5 Add the blue cheese, cream and basil. Transfer to a food processor or blender and process until smooth, working in batches if necessary. Taste and adjust the seasoning.

6 Reheat the soup, but do not boil. Ladle into bowls and garnish with the crumbled bacon and basil.

Corn and Crab Chowder

Chowder comes from the French word *chaudron* meaning a large cooking pot. This is what the fishermen on the east coast of the United States used for boiling up whatever was left over from their catch for supper.

INGREDIENTS

Serves 4

2 tbsp butter
1 small onion, chopped
12oz can corn kernels, drained
2½ cups milk
6oz can white crabmeat, drained
   and flaked
1 cup cooked, peeled shrimp
2 scallions, finely chopped
⅔ cup light cream
pinch of cayenne pepper
salt and black pepper
4 whole shrimp in shells, to garnish

1 Melt the butter in a large saucepan and gently fry the onion for 4–5 minutes, until softened.

2 Reserve 2 tbsp of the corn for the garnish and add the remainder to the pan with the milk. Bring the soup to a boil, then reduce the heat, cover the pan and simmer over a low heat for 5 minutes.

3 Pour the soup, in several batches if necessary, into a blender or food processor and whizz until smooth.

4 Return the soup to the pan and stir in the crabmeat, shrimp, scallions, cream and cayenne pepper. Reheat gently over a low heat.

5 Meanwhile, place the reserved corn kernels in a small frying pan without oil and dry-fry over a medium heat until golden and toasted.

6 Season the soup well and serve each bowlful topped with a few of the toasted kernels and a whole shrimp.

Pea and Ham Broth

INGREDIENTS

Serves 8

2½ cups dried green or yellow split
   peas
8 cups water
1 ham bone with some meat left on it,
   or 1 ham hock
1 onion, finely chopped
1 leek, sliced
2 celery stalks, finely sliced
a few fresh parsley sprigs
6 black peppercorns
2 bay leaves
salt
flat-leaf parsley, to garnish

1 Rinse the split peas under cold running water. Place the peas in a large pan and add water to cover. Bring to a boil and boil for 2 minutes. Remove the pan from the heat and leave to soak for 1 hour. Drain.

2 Return the peas to the pan and add the measured water, ham bone or hock, onion, leeks, celery, a couple of sprigs of parsley, salt, peppercorns and bay leaves. Bring to a boil, then reduce the heat, cover and simmer gently for 1–1½ hours, until the peas are tender. Skim occasionally.

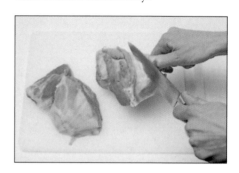

3 Remove the bay leaves and the ham bone or hock from the soup. Cut the meat off the bone, discarding any fat and chop the meat into small cubes. Set the meat aside. Discard the ham bone and the bay leaves.

4 Purée the soup in batches in a food processor or blender. Pour into a clean saucepan and add the chopped ham. Check the seasoning. Simmer the soup for 3–4 minutes to heat through before serving. Garnish with parsley.

Turkey and Lentil Soup

INGREDIENTS

Serves 4

2 tbsp butter or margarine
1 large carrot, chopped
1 onion, chopped
1 leek, white part only, chopped
1 celery stalk, chopped
4oz mushrooms, chopped
3 tbsp dry white wine
4 cups chicken stock
2 tsp dried thyme
1 bay leaf
½ cup brown or green lentils
8oz cooked turkey, diced
salt and black pepper

1 Melt the butter or margarine in a large saucepan. Add the carrot, onion, leek, celery and mushrooms. Cook for 3–5 minutes, until softened.

2 Stir in the wine and chicken stock. Bring to a boil and skim off any foam that rises to the surface. Add the thyme and bay leaf. Reduce the heat, cover, and simmer for 30 minutes.

3 Add the lentils and continue cooking, covered, for 30–40 minutes more, until they are just tender. Stir the soup from time to time.

4 Stir in the diced turkey and season to taste with salt and pepper. Cook until just heated through. Ladle the soup into bowls and serve hot.

COLD STARTERS

Chilled starters are often thought of as summer food, though they make a light and refreshing start to a meal at any time of the year. Fruity combinations such as Minted Melon Salad, or Prosciutto with Mango are especially good to serve before a rich main course. While fish dishes, such as Potted Shrimp, and Smoked Haddock Pâté are best followed by lighter foods. Leeks, served cold with a mustard dressing, or marinated in walnut dressing, make a delicious change in winter, and goat cheese, either marinated or broiled is good with almost anything.

Egg and Tomato Salad with Crab

INGREDIENTS

Serves 4

1 round lettuce
2 x 7oz cans crabmeat, drained
4 hard boiled eggs, sliced
16 cherry tomatoes, halved
½ green bell pepper, seeded and
  thinly sliced
6 pitted black olives, sliced

For the dressing

1 cup mayonnaise
2 tsp fresh lemon juice
3 tbsp chili sauce
½ green bell pepper, seeded and
  finely chopped
1 tsp horseradish cream
1 tsp Worcestershire sauce

1 To make the dressing, place all the ingredients in a bowl and mix well. Set aside in a cool place.

2 Line four plates with the lettuce leaves. Mound the crabmeat in the center. Arrange the eggs around the outside with the tomatoes on top.

3 Spoon some of the dressing over the crabmeat. Arrange the green pepper slices on top and sprinkle with the olives. Serve immediately with the remaining dressing.

Summer Tuna Salad

INGREDIENTS

Serves 4–6

6oz radishes
1 cucumber
3 celery stalks
1 yellow bell pepper
6oz cherry tomatoes, halved
4 thinly sliced scallions
3 tbsp lemon juice
3 tbsp olive oil
2 x 7oz cans tuna, drained and flaked
2 tbsp chopped fresh parsley
salt and black pepper
lettuce leaves, to serve
thin strips twisted lemon rind,
  to garnish

1 Cut the radishes, cucumber, celery and yellow pepper into small cubes. Place in a large, shallow dish with the cherry tomatoes and scallions.

2 In a small bowl, stir together the salt and lemon juice with a fork, until dissolved. Pour this over the vegetable mixture. Add the oil and pepper to taste. Stir to coat the vegetables. Cover and set aside for 1 hour.

3 Add the flaked tuna and parsley to the mixture and toss gently until well combined.

4 Arrange the lettuce leaves on a platter and spoon the salad into the center. Garnish with the lemon rind.

> —— VARIATION ——
>
> Prepare the vegetables as above and add the parsley. Arrange lettuce leaves on individual plates and divide the vegetable mixture among them. Place a mound of tuna on top of each and finish with a dollop of mayonnaise.

Leek Terrine with Deli Meats

This attractive appetizer is very simple to make yet looks spectacular. You can make the terrine a day ahead and keep it covered in the refrigerator. If your guests are vegetarian offer chunks of feta cheese.

INGREDIENTS

Serves 6
20–24 small young leeks
4 tbsp walnut oil
4 tbsp olive oil
2 tbsp white wine vinegar
1 tsp whole grain mustard
about 8oz mixed sliced meats, such as prosciutto, Genoa salami or mortadella
²⁄₃ cup walnuts, toasted and chopped
salt and black pepper

1 Cut off the roots and most of the green part from the leeks. Wash them thoroughly under cold running water to get rid of any grit or mud.

2 Bring a large pan of salted water to a boil. Add the leeks, bring the water back to a boil, then reduce the heat and simmer for 6–8 minutes, until the leeks are just tender. Drain well.

3 Fill a 1lb loaf pan with the leeks, placing them alternately head to tail and sprinkling each layer as you go with salt and pepper.

4 Put another loaf pan inside the first and gently press down on the leeks. Carefully invert both pans and let any water drain out.

5 Place one or two weights on top of the pans and chill the terrine for at least 4 hours, or overnight.

6 Meanwhile, make the dressing. Whisk together the walnut and olive oils, vinegar and whole grain mustard in a small bowl. Add seasoning to taste.

7 Carefully turn out the terrine on to a board and cut into slices using a large sharp knife. Lay the slices of leek terrine on serving plates and arrange the slices of meat alongside.

8 Spoon the dressing over the slices of terrine and scatter over the chopped walnuts. Serve at once.

— COOK'S TIP —

For this terrine, it is important to use tender young leeks. The white part mainly is used in this recipe, but the green tops can be used in soups. The terrine must be pressed for at least 4 hours – this makes it easier to carve into slices. You can vary the sliced meats as you like. Try smoked beef, salami, smoked venison or baked ham for a change.

— VARIATION —

If you are short of time, serve the cooked leeks simply marinated in the walnut and mustard dressing.

Avocado and Paw Paw Salad

INGREDIENTS

Serves 4

2 ripe avocados
1 ripe paw paw
1 large orange
1 small red onion
1–2oz small arugula leaves or lamb's
    lettuce

For the dressing

4 tbsp olive oil
2 tbsp fresh lemon or lime juice
salt and black pepper

1 Halve the avocados and remove the pits. Carefully peel off the skin, then cut each avocado half lengthwise into thick slices.

2 Peel the paw paw. Cut it in half lengthwise and scoop out the seeds with a spoon. Set aside 1 tsp of the seeds for the dressing. Cut each paw paw half lengthwise into eight slices.

3 Peel the orange. Using a small sharp knife, cut out the segments, cutting either side of the dividing membranes. Cut the onion into very thin slices and separate into rings.

4 Combine the dressing ingredients in a small bowl and mix well. Stir in the reserved paw paw seeds.

5 Assemble the salad on four individual serving plates. Alternate slices of paw paw and avocado. Add the orange segments and a small mound of arugula or lamb's lettuce topped with onion rings. Spoon over the dressing.

Asparagus with Creamy Vinaigrette

INGREDIENTS

Serves 4

1½lb asparagus spears
2 tbsp raspberry vinegar
½ tsp salt
1 tsp Dijon mustard
5 tbsp sunflower oil
2 tbsp sour cream or natural yogurt
white pepper
6oz fresh raspberries

1 Fill a large shallow saucepan with water – it needs to be about 4in deep. Bring to a boil.

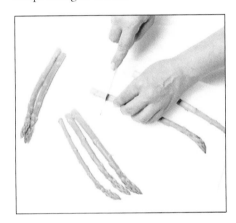

2 Trim off the tough ends from the asparagus spears. You may need to remove 1–2in from each spear.

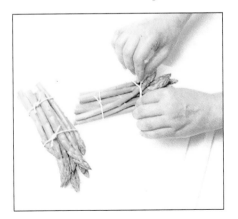

3 Tie the asparagus spears into two bundles. Lower the bundles into the boiling water and cook for 5–7 minutes, until just tender.

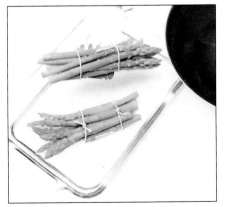

4 Carefully remove the asparagus bundles from the boiling water and immediately immerse them in cold water to prevent further cooking. Drain and untie the bundles. Pat dry the spears with paper towels. Chill the asparagus for at least 1 hour.

5 Place the vinegar and salt in a bowl and stir with a fork until the salt is dissolved. Stir in the mustard, then gradually whisk in the oil until blended. Add the sour cream or yogurt and pepper to taste.

6 To serve, arrange the asparagus spears on individual plates and drizzle the dressing across the middle of the spears. Garnish with the fresh raspberries and serve at once.

Minted Melon Salad

This appetizer is nicest made with two different kinds of melon; choose from an orange-fleshed Cantaloupe, a pale green Crenshaw, or a sweet white-fleshed Honeydew.

INGREDIENTS

Serves 4
2 ripe melons

For the dressing
2 tbsp roughly chopped fresh mint
1 tsp sugar
2 tbsp raspberry vinegar
6 tbsp extra virgin olive oil
salt and black pepper
mint sprigs, to decorate

1 Halve the melons, then scoop out the seeds using a dessert spoon. Cut the melons into thin wedges using a large sharp knife and remove the skins.

2 Arrange the two different varieties of melon wedges alternately on four individual serving plates.

3 To make the dressing, whisk together the mint, sugar, vinegar, oil and seasoning in a small bowl, or put in a screw-top jar and shake until blended.

4 Spoon the mint dressing over the melon wedges and decorate with mint sprigs. Serve very lightly chilled.

Marinated Goat Cheese with Herbs

These little cheeses are delicious spread on toasted slices of French bread, brushed with olive oil and rubbed with garlic.

INGREDIENTS

Serves 4–8
4 fresh soft goat cheeses
6 tbsp chopped fresh mixed parsley, thyme and oregano
2 garlic cloves, chopped
12 black peppercorns, lightly crushed
²⁄₃ cup extra virgin olive oil
salad leaves such as green leaf or oak leaf lettuce, to serve

---
COOK'S TIP

Any herbs can be added to the marinade – try chervil, tarragon, chives and basil. If you prefer, reserve the herb-flavored oil, and use it to make a salad dressing.

---

1 Arrange the fresh goat cheeses in a single layer in a large shallow non-metallic dish.

2 Put the chopped herbs, garlic and crushed peppercorns in a blender or food processor. Start the machine, then pour in the oil and process until the mixture is fairly smooth.

3 Spoon the herb mixture over the cheeses, then cover and leave to marinate in the fridge for 24 hours, basting the cheeses occasionally.

4 Remove the cheeses from the fridge about 30 minutes before serving and allow them to come back to room temperature. Serve the cheeses on a bed of salad leaves and spoon over a little of the olive oil and herb mixture.

Pears and Blue Cheese

Stilton is the classic blue-veined cheese, but you could use any flavorful, creamy blue cheese, such as Gorgonzola.

INGREDIENTS

Serves 4
4 ripe pears, lightly chilled
3oz blue cheese
2oz medium fat soft cheese
pepper
watercress sprigs, to garnish

For the dressing
3 tbsp light olive oil
1 tbsp lemon juice
½ tbsp toasted poppy seeds
salt and black pepper

1 First make the dressing, place the olive oil, lemon juice, poppy seeds and seasoning in a screw-topped jar and shake together until emulsified.

2 Cut the pears in half lengthwise, then scoop out the cores and cut away the calyx from the rounded end.

3 Beat together the blue cheese, soft cheese and a little pepper and divide among the cavities in the pears.

4 Shake the dressing to mix it again, then spoon it over the pears. Serve garnished with watercress.

Potted Shrimp

The tiny brown shrimp that are traditionally used for potting are very fiddly to peel – it is easier to use peeled, cooked shrimp instead.

INGREDIENTS

Serves 4
8oz shelled shrimp
1 cup butter
pinch of ground mace
salt
cayenne pepper
dill sprigs, to garnish
lemon wedges and thin slices of brown
   bread and butter, to serve

1 Chop a quarter of the shrimp. Melt ½ cup of the butter slowly, carefully skimming off any foam that rises to the surface.

2 Stir all the shrimp, the mace, salt and cayenne into the pan and heat gently without boiling. Pour the shrimp and butter mixture into four individual pots and leave to cool.

3 Heat the remaining butter in a clean small saucepan, then carefully spoon the clear butter over the shrimp, leaving behind the sediment.

4 Leave until the butter is almost set, then place a dill sprig in the center of each pot. Leave to set completely, then cover and chill.

5 Transfer the shrimp to room temperature 30 minutes before serving with lemon wedges and thin slices of brown bread and butter.

Melon and Crab Salad

INGREDIENTS

Serves 6

1lb fresh crabmeat
½ cup mayonnaise
3 tbsp sour cream or natural
 yogurt
2 tbsp olive oil
2 tbsp fresh lemon or lime juice
2–3 scallions, finely chopped
2 tbsp finely chopped fresh
 coriander
¼ tsp cayenne pepper
salt and black pepper
1½ cantaloupe or small honeydew
 melons
3 medium Belgian endive heads
fresh coriander sprigs, to garnish

1 Pick over the crabmeat very carefully, removing any bits of shell or cartilage. Leave the pieces of crabmeat as large as possible.

2 In a medium-size bowl, combine all the other ingredients except the melons and endive, and mix well. Fold the crabmeat into this dressing.

3 Halve the melons and remove and discard the seeds. Cut them into thin slices, then remove the rind.

4 Arrange the salad on six individual serving plates, making a decorative design with the melon slices and whole endive leaves. Place a mound of dressed crabmeat on each plate and garnish the salads with one or two fresh coriander sprigs.

Smoked Trout Salad

Horseradish is as good a partner to smoked trout as it is to roast beef. In this recipe it combines with yogurt to make a delicious light salad dressing.

INGREDIENTS

Serves 4
1 oakleaf or other red lettuce
8oz small tomatoes, cut into thin
    wedges
½ cucumber, peeled and thinly sliced
4 smoked trout fillets, about
    7oz each, skinned and flaked

For the dressing
pinch of English mustard powder
3–4 tsp white wine vinegar
2 tbsp light olive oil
scant ½ cup natural yogurt
about 2 tbsp grated fresh or
    bottled horseradish
pinch of sugar

1 First, make the dressing. Mix together the mustard powder and vinegar, then gradually whisk in the oil, yogurt, horseradish and sugar. Set aside for 30 minutes.

COOK'S TIP

Additional salt should not be necessary in this recipe because of the saltiness of the smoked trout.

2 Place the lettuce leaves in a large bowl. Stir the dressing again, then pour half of it over the leaves and toss lightly using two spoons.

3 Arrange the lettuce on four individual plates with the tomatoes, cucumber and trout. Spoon over the remaining dressing and serve at once.

Melon and Grapefruit Cocktail

This pretty, colorful starter can be made in minutes, so it is perfect for when you don't have time to cook, but want something really special to eat.

INGREDIENTS 🍎

Serves 4
1 small Ogen melon
1 small Charentais melon
2 pink grapefruit
3 tbsp orange juice
4 tbsp red vermouth
seeds from ½ pomegranate
mint sprigs, to decorate

COOK'S TIP

To check if the melons are ripe, smell them – they should have a heady aroma. They should also give slightly when pressed at the stalk end.

---

1 Halve the melons lengthwise and scoop out all the seeds. Cut into wedges and remove the skins, then cut across into large bite-sized pieces.

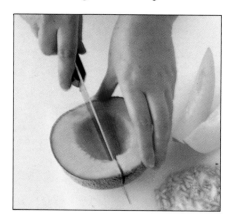

2 Using a small sharp knife, cut the peel and pith from the grapefruit. Holding the fruit over a bowl to catch the juice, cut between the grapefruit membranes to release the segments. Set aside the grapefruit segments.

3 Stir the orange juice and vermouth into the reserved grapefruit juice.

4 Arrange the melon pieces and grapefruit segments haphazardly on four individual serving plates. Spoon over the dressing, then scatter with the pomegranate seeds. Decorate with mint sprigs and serve at once.

Prosciutto with Mango

Other fresh, colorful fruits, such as figs, paw paw or melon would go equally well with the prosciutto in this light, elegant starter. It is amazingly simple to prepare and can be made in advance – ideal if you are serving a complicated main course.

INGREDIENTS 🍎

Serves 4
16 slices prosciutto
1 ripe mango
black pepper
flat leaf parsley sprigs, to garnish

1 Separate the prosciutto slices and arrange four on each of four individual plates, crumpling the meat slightly to give a decorative effect.

2 Cut the mango into three thick slices around the pit, then slice the flesh and discard the pit. Neatly cut away the skin from each slice.

3 Arrange the mango slices in among the prosciutto. Grind over some black pepper and serve garnished with flat leaf parsley sprigs.

Feta Tabbouleh in Radicchio Cups

The radicchio cups are simply a presentation idea. If you prefer, spoon the bulgur wheat mixture on to a serving plate lined with Romaine lettuce leaves.

INGREDIENTS

Serves 4
generous ⅓ cup bulgur wheat
4 tbsp olive oil
juice of 1 lemon, or more to taste
4 scallions, chopped
6 tbsp chopped flat leaf parsley
3 tbsp chopped fresh mint
2 tomatoes, peeled, seeded and diced
6oz feta cheese, cubed
salt and black pepper
1 head radicchio
flat leaf parsley sprigs, to garnish

1 Soak the bulgur wheat in cold water for 1 hour. Drain thoroughly in a sieve and press out the excess water.

2 Mix together the oil, lemon juice and seasoning in a bowl. Add the bulgur wheat, then mix well, making sure all the grains are coated with the dressing. Leave at room temperature for about 15 minutes so the bulgur wheat can absorb some of the flavors.

3 Stir in the scallions, parsley, mint, tomatoes and feta. Taste and adjust the seasoning, adding more lemon juice to sharpen the flavor, if necessary.

4 Separate out the leaves from the radicchio and select the best cup-shaped ones. Spoon a little of the tabbouleh into each one. Arrange on individual plates or on a serving platter and garnish with flat leaf parsley sprigs.

Bresaola, Onion and Arugula Salad

INGREDIENTS

Serves 4
2 medium onions, peeled
5–6 tbsp olive oil
juice of 1 lemon
12 thin slices bresaola
2–3oz arugula
salt and black pepper

1 Slice each onion into eight wedges through the root.

2 Arrange the onion wedges in a single layer on a broiling rack or in a flameproof dish. Brush them with a little of the olive oil and season well with salt and pepper to taste.

3 Place the onion wedges under a hot broiler and cook for about 8–10 minutes, turning once, until they are just beginning to soften and turn golden brown at the edges.

4 Meanwhile, to make the dressing, mix together the lemon juice and 4 tbsp of the olive oil in a small bowl. Add salt and black pepper to taste and whisk well until the dressing is thoroughly blended.

5 If you have broiled the onions on a broiling rack, transfer them to a shallow dish once they are cooked.

6 Pour the lemon dressing over the hot onions and leave until cold.

7 When the onions are cold, arrange the bresaola slices on individual serving plates with the onions and arugula. Spoon over any remaining dressing and serve at once.

Leeks with Mustard Dressing

Pencil-slim baby leeks are increasingly available nowadays, and are beautifully tender. Use three or four of these smaller leeks per serving.

INGREDIENTS

Serves 4

8 slim leeks, each about 5in long
1–2 tsp Dijon mustard
2 tsp white wine vinegar
1 hard boiled egg, halved lengthwise
5 tbsp light olive oil
2 tsp chopped fresh parsley
salt and black pepper

1 Steam the leeks over a pan of boiling water until just tender.

2 Meanwhile, stir together the mustard and vinegar in a bowl. Scoop the egg yolk into the bowl and mash thoroughly into the vinegar mixture using a fork.

3 Gradually work in the oil to make a smooth sauce, then season to taste.

4 Lift the leeks out of the steamer and place on several layers of paper towels, then cover the leeks with several more layers of paper towels and pat dry.

5 Transfer the leeks to a serving dish while still warm, spoon the dressing over them and leave to cool. Finely chop the egg white using a large sharp knife, then mix with the chopped fresh parsley and scatter over the leeks. Chill until ready to serve.

--- COOK'S TIP ---

Although this dish is served cold, make sure that the leeks are still warm when you pour over the dressing so that they will absorb the mustardy flavors.

Smoked Haddock Pâté

Arbroath smokies are small haddock that are beheaded and gutted but not split before being salted and hot-smoked. Use 1½lb smoked haddock fillet, if you prefer.

INGREDIENTS

Serves 6
3 Arbroath smokies, about 8oz each
1¼ cups medium fat soft cheese
3 eggs, beaten
2–3 tbsp lemon juice
pepper
sprigs of chervil, to garnish
lemon wedges and lettuce leaves,
   to serve

1 Preheat the oven to 325°F. Butter six ramekin dishes.

2 Lay the smokies in a baking dish and heat through in the oven for 10 minutes. Carefully remove the skin and bones from the smokies, then flake the flesh into a bowl.

COOK'S TIP

There should be no need to add salt to this recipe, as smoked haddock is naturally salty – taste the mixture to check.

3 Mash the fish with a fork and work in the cheese, then the eggs. Add lemon juice and pepper to taste.

4 Divide the fish mixture among the ramekins and place in a roasting pan. Pour hot water into the roasting pan to come halfway up the dishes. Bake for 30 minutes, until just set.

5 Allow to cool for 2–3 minutes, then run a knife point around the edge of each dish and invert on to a warmed plate. Garnish with chervil sprigs and serve with the lemon and lettuce.

French Goat Cheese Salad

INGREDIENTS

Serves 4

7oz bag prepared mixed salad leaves
4 strips bacon
16 thin slices French bread
4oz goat cheese

For the dressing

4 tbsp olive oil
1 tbsp tarragon vinegar
2 tsp walnut oil
1 tsp Dijon mustard
1 tsp whole grain mustard

1 Preheat the broiler to a medium heat. Rinse and dry the salad leaves, then arrange in four individual bowls. Place the ingredients for the dressing in a screw-topped jar, shake together well and reserve.

2 Lay the bacon strips on a board, then stretch with the back of a knife and cut each into four. Roll each piece up and broil for about 2–3 minutes.

3 Meanwhile, slice the goat cheese into eight and halve each slice. Top each slice of bread with a piece of goat cheese and pop under the broiler. Turn over the bacon and continue cooking with the goat cheese toasts until the cheese is golden and bubbling.

4 Arrange the bacon rolls and toasts on top of the prepared salad leaves, shake the dressing well and pour a little of the dressing over each one.

COOK'S TIP

If you prefer, just slice the goat cheese and place on toasted French bread. Or use whole wheat toast for a delicious nutty flavor.

Greek Salad Pitas

Horiatiki is the Greek name for this classic salad made with feta – a cheese made from sheeps' milk. Try serving the salad in hot pita breads with a minty yogurt dressing.

INGREDIENTS

Makes 4

1 cup diced feta cheese
¼ cucumber, peeled and diced
8 cherry tomatoes, quartered
½ small green bell pepper, seeded and thinly sliced
¼ small onion, thinly sliced
8 black olives, pitted and halved
2 tbsp olive oil
1 tsp dried oregano
4 large pita breads
4 tbsp natural yogurt
1 tsp dried mint
salt and black pepper
fresh mint, to garnish

1 Place the cheese, cucumber, tomatoes, pepper, onion and olives in a bowl. Stir in the olive oil and oregano, then season well and reserve.

2 Place the pita breads in a toaster or under a preheated broiler for about 2 minutes, until puffed up. Meanwhile, to make the dressing, mix the yogurt with the mint, season well and reserve.

3 Holding the hot pitas in a dish towel, slice each one from top to bottom down one of the longest sides and open out to form a pocket.

4 Divide the prepared salad among the pita breads and drizzle over a spoonful of the dressing. Serve the pitas immediately, garnished with the fresh mint.

HOT STARTERS

In cooler weather, hot starters come into their own, and crumbly, creamy shellfish gratins, Deviled Kidneys, and Baked Eggs with Tarragon are all traditional winter fare. A few dishes, such as Herb Omelette with Tomato Salad, are even substantial enough to make a light lunch-time meal. However hot starters aren't necessarily rich and filling; lighter, contemporary recipes such as mini kabobs made with mussels and scallops, Spinach Salad with Bacon and Shrimp, and Hot Tomato and Mozzarella Salad are perfect before a filling main course.

Creamy Creole Crab

INGREDIENTS

Serves 6

2 x 7oz cans crabmeat
3 hard boiled eggs
1 tsp Dijon mustard
6 tbsp butter or margarine, at room
   temperature
¼ tsp cayenne pepper
3 tbsp sherry
2 tbsp chopped fresh parsley
½ cup light or whipping cream
2–3 thinly sliced scallions including
   some of the green parts
½ cup dried white bread crumbs
salt and black pepper

1 Preheat the oven to 350°F. Flake the crabmeat into a medium-size bowl, keeping the pieces of crab as large as possible and removing any shell or cartilage.

2 In a medium-size bowl, crumble the egg yolks with a fork. Add the mustard, 4 tbsp of the butter or margarine and the cayenne pepper, then mash together to form a paste. Mix in the sherry and parsley.

3 Chop the egg whites and mix in with the cream and scallions. Stir in the crabmeat and season well.

4 Divide the crab mixture equally among six greased scallop shells or individual baking dishes. Sprinkle with the bread crumbs and dot with the remaining butter or margarine.

5 Bake for about 20 minutes, until bubbling hot and golden brown.

Scallop and Mussel Kabobs

INGREDIENTS

Serves 4

5 tbsp butter, at room temperature
2 tbsp finely chopped fresh fennel
    fronds or parsley
1 tbsp fresh lemon juice
32 small scallops
24 large mussels in the shell
8 bacon slices
1 cup fresh white bread crumbs
3 tbsp olive oil
salt and black pepper
parsley sprigs and lemon peel,
    to garnish
hot toast, to serve

1 Make the flavored butter by combining the butter with the chopped herbs, lemon juice and salt and pepper to taste. Mix well. Set aside.

2 In a small saucepan, cook the scallops in their own liquid for about 5 minutes, or until just tender. (If there is no scallop liquid – retained from the shells after shucking – use a little fish stock or white wine.) Drain and pat dry with paper towels.

3 Scrub the mussels well, discarding any broken ones, and rinse under cold running water. Place in a large saucepan with about 1in of water. Cover the pan and steam the mussels over a medium heat until they open. Remove them from their shells, and pat dry on paper towels. Discard any mussels that have not opened.

4 Thread four scallops, three mussels and a slice of bacon on to eight 6in wooden or metal skewers, weaving the bacon between the scallops and mussels as you thread them.

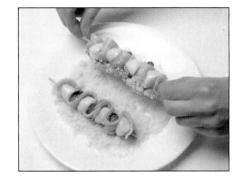

5 Preheat the broiler. Spread out the bread crumbs on a plate. Brush the seafood with olive oil and roll in the crumbs to coat all over.

6 Place the skewers on the broiler rack. Broil for 4–5 minutes on each side until crisp and lightly browned. Serve immediately garnished with the parsley sprigs and lemon peel and accompanied by hot toast and the flavored butter.

Goat Cheese Tarts

INGREDIENTS

Serves 6

6–8 sheets filo pastry (about 4oz)
4 tbsp butter, melted
12oz firm goat cheese
9 cherry tomatoes, quartered
½ cup milk
2 eggs
2 tbsp light cream
large pinch of white pepper

COOK'S TIP

Keep the filo pastry under a damp cloth while working to prevent the sheets from drying out.

---

1 First, preheat the oven to 375°F. Grease six 4in tartlet pans.

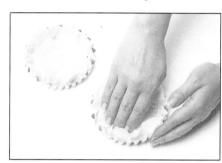

2 Then make the pie shells. For each pan, cut out four rounds of filo pastry, each about 4½in in diameter. Place one round in the pan and brush with butter. Top with another filo round and continue until there are four layers of filo; do not butter the last layer. Repeat for the remaining pans.

3 Place the pastry-lined pans on a baking sheet. Cut the goat cheese log into six slices and place a slice of cheese in each of the pie shells.

4 Arrange the tomato quarters around the goat cheese slices.

5 Place the milk, eggs, cream and pepper in a measuring cup or bowl and whisk to mix. Pour into the pie shells, filling them almost to the top.

6 Bake in the oven for 30–40 minutes, until puffed and golden. Serve hot or warm, with a mixed green salad if desired.

Baked Eggs with Tarragon

Traditional *cocotte* dishes or small ramekins can be used for this recipe, as either will take one egg perfectly.

INGREDIENTS

Serves 4
3 tbsp butter
½ cup heavy cream
1–2 tbsp chopped fresh
   tarragon
4 eggs
salt and black pepper
fresh tarragon sprigs, to garnish

1 Preheat the oven to 350°F. Lightly butter four small ovenproof dishes, then warm them up in the oven for a few minutes.

2 Meanwhile, gently warm the cream. Sprinkle some tarragon into each dish, then spoon in a little of the cream.

3 Carefully break an egg into each of the prepared ovenproof dishes, season the eggs with salt and pepper and spoon a little more of the cream over each of the eggs.

4 Add a knob of butter to each dish and place them in a roasting pan containing sufficient water to come halfway up the sides of the dishes. Bake for 8–10 minutes, until the whites are just set and the yolks still soft. Serve hot, garnished with tarragon sprigs.

Herb Omelette with Tomato Salad

This is ideal as a starter before a light main course – use flavorful, fresh plum tomatoes in season.

INGREDIENTS

Serves 4

4 eggs, beaten
2 tbsp chopped, mixed fresh herbs, such as chives, marjoram, thyme or parsley, or 2 tsp dried
1 tbsp butter
3–4 tbsp olive oil
1 tbsp fresh orange juice
1 tsp red wine vinegar
1 tsp grainy mustard
2 large tomatoes, thinly sliced
salt and black pepper
fresh herb sprigs, to garnish

1 Beat the eggs, herbs and seasoning together. Heat the butter and a little of the oil in an omelette pan.

2 When the fats are just sizzling, pour in the egg mixture and leave to set, stirring very occasionally with a fork. This omelette needs to be almost cooked through (about 5 minutes).

3 Meanwhile, heat the rest of the oil in a small pan with the orange juice, vinegar and mustard, and add salt and pepper to taste.

4 Roll up the cooked omelette and neatly cut into ½in wide strips. Keep them rolled up and transfer immediately to the hot plates.

5 Arrange the sliced tomatoes on the plates with the omelette rolls and pour on the warm dressing. Garnish with herb sprigs and serve at once.

Three-cheese Croûtes

INGREDIENTS

Serves 2–4

4 thick slices of slightly stale bread
little butter, or mustard
3oz Brie
3 tbsp ricotta
2oz grated Parmesan or mature Cheddar
1 small garlic clove, crushed
salt and black pepper
black olives, to garnish

—— COOK'S TIP ——

If you have Brie which will not ripen fully, this is an excellent way of using it up. You'll need a knife and fork to eat this tasty appetizer.

1 Preheat the oven to 400°F. Place the bread slices on a baking sheet, close together, and spread with either a little butter or mustard.

2 Cut the Brie into thin slices or pieces and arrange the slices or pieces evenly on the bread.

3 Mix together the ricotta, Parmesan or Cheddar, garlic, and seasoning to taste. Spread over the Brie and the bread to the corners.

4 Bake for 10–15 minutes, or until golden and bubbling. Serve immediately, garnished with black olives.

Spinach Salad with Bacon and Shrimp

Serve this hot salad with plenty of crusty bread for mopping up the delicious juices.

INGREDIENTS

Serves 4
7 tbsp olive oil
2 tbsp sherry vinegar
2 garlic cloves, finely chopped
1 tsp Dijon mustard
12 cooked jumbo shrimp
4oz lean bacon, rinded and cut into
 strips
about 4oz fresh young spinach
 leaves
½ head oak leaf lettuce, roughly torn
salt and black pepper

1 To make the dressing, whisk together 6 tbsp of the olive oil with the vinegar, garlic, mustard and season-ing in a small pan. Heat gently until thickened slightly, then keep warm.

2 Carefully peel the shrimp, leaving the tails intact. Set aside.

3 Heat the remaining oil in a frying pan and fry the bacon until golden and crisp, stirring occasionally. Add the shrimp and stir-fry for a few minutes until warmed through.

4 While the bacon and shrimp are cooking, arrange the spinach and torn oak leaf lettuce leaves on four individual serving plates.

5 Spoon the bacon and shrimp on to the leaves, then pour over the hot dressing. Serve at once.

--- COOK'S TIP ---

Sherry vinegar lends its pungent flavor to this delicious salad. You can buy it from larger supermarkets and gourmet stores.

Mussels with Cream and Parsley

INGREDIENTS

Serves 2

1½lb mussels in the shell
½ fennel bulb, finely chopped
1 shallot, finely chopped
3 tbsp dry white wine
3 tbsp light cream
2 tbsp chopped fresh parsley
freshly ground black pepper

1 Scrub the mussels under cold running water. Remove any barnacles with a small knife and tear away the beards. Rinse once more.

2 Place the mussels in a large wide pan with a lid. Sprinkle them with the fennel, shallot and wine. Cover and place over a medium-high heat shaking the pan occasionally. Steam for 3–5 minutes, until the mussels open.

3 Lift out the mussels with a slotted spoon and remove the top shells. Discard any that did not open. Arrange the mussels, on their bottom shells, in one layer in a shallow serving dish. Cover and keep warm in a low oven.

4 Place a double layer of dampened cheesecloth or a clean dish towel in a sieve set over a bowl. Strain the mussel cooking liquid through the cloth or towel. Return the liquid to a clean saucepan and bring to a boil.

5 Add the cream, stir well and boil for 3 minutes to reduce slightly, then stir in the parsley. Spoon the sauce over the mussels and sprinkle with freshly ground black pepper. Serve the mussels immediately.

Cheese and Spinach Puffs

INGREDIENTS

Serves 6

1 cup cooked, chopped spinach
¾ cup cottage cheese
1 tsp ground nutmeg
2 egg whites
2 tbsp grated Parmesan cheese
salt and black pepper

1 Preheat the oven to 425°F. Brush six ramekin dishes with oil.

2 Mix together the spinach and cottage cheese in a small bowl, then add the nutmeg and seasoning to taste.

3 Whisk the egg whites in a separate bowl until stiff enough to hold soft peaks. Fold them evenly into the spinach mixture using a spatula or large metal spoon, then spoon the mixture into the oiled ramekins, dividing it evenly, and smooth the tops.

4 Sprinkle with the Parmesan and place on a baking sheet. Bake for 15–20 minutes, or until puffed and golden brown. Serve immediately.

--- COOK'S TIP ---

Make sure that the spinach is not too wet. Tip it into a strainer and press firmly with the back of a wooden spoon to squeeze out the excess liquid.

Lemony Stuffed Zucchini

INGREDIENTS

Serves 4

4 zucchini, about 6oz each
1 tsp sunflower oil
1 garlic clove, crushed
1 tsp ground lemongrass
finely grated rind and juice of ½ lemon
scant ¾ cup cooked long grain rice
6oz cherry tomatoes, halved
2 tbsp toasted cashews
salt and black pepper
sprigs of thyme, to garnish

--- VARIATIONS ---

Other cooked grains would be equally good in this dish, try bulgur wheat, couscous or whole grain rice.

1 Preheat the oven to 400°F. Halve the zucchini lengthwise and use a teaspoon to scoop out the centers. Blanch the shells in boiling water for 1 minute, then drain well.

2 Chop the zucchini flesh finely and place in a saucepan with the oil and garlic. Stir over moderate heat until softened, but not browned.

3 Stir in the lemongrass, lemon rind and juice, rice, tomatoes, and cashews. Season well and spoon into the zucchini shells. Place the shells in a baking pan and cover with foil.

4 Bake for 25–30 minutes or until the zucchini is tender, then serve hot, garnished with thyme sprigs.

Chinese Garlic Mushrooms

Tofu is high in protein and very low in fat, so it is a very useful food to keep handy and, it makes a tasty stuffing for mushrooms.

INGREDIENTS 🍎

Serves 4

8 large open cup mushrooms
3 scallions, sliced
1 garlic clove, crushed
2 tbsp oyster sauce
10oz packet marinated tofu, cut into
   small dice
7oz can corn, drained
2 tsp sesame oil
salt and black pepper

1 Preheat the oven to 400°F. Finely chop the mushroom stalks and mix with the scallions, garlic, and oyster sauce.

2 Stir in the diced marinated tofu and corn, season well with salt and pepper, then carefully spoon the filling into the mushrooms.

3 Brush the edges of the mushrooms with the sesame oil. Arrange the stuffed mushrooms in a baking dish and bake for 12–15 minutes, until the mushrooms are just tender, then serve at once.

— COOK'S TIP —

If you prefer, omit the oyster sauce and use light soy sauce instead.

Deviled Kidneys

'Deviled' dishes are always hot and spicy. If you have time, mix the spicy ingredients together in advance to give the flavors time to mingle and mature.

INGREDIENTS

Serves 4
2 tsp Worcestershire sauce
1 tbsp prepared English mustard
1 tbsp lemon juice
1 tbsp tomato paste
pinch of cayenne pepper
3 tbsp butter
1 shallot, finely chopped
8 lamb's kidneys, skinned, halved
   and cored
salt and black pepper
1 tbsp chopped fresh parsley,
   to garnish

1 Mix the Worcestershire sauce, mustard, lemon juice, tomato paste, cayenne pepper and salt together to make a sauce.

2 Melt the butter in a frying pan, add the shallot and cook, stirring occasionally, until softened but not colored.

— COOK'S TIP —

To remove the cores from the lamb's kidneys, use kitchen scissors, rather than a knife – you will find that it is much easier.

3 Stir the kidney halves into the shallot in the pan and cook over a medium-high heat for about 3 minutes on each side.

4 Pour the sauce over the kidneys and quickly stir so they are evenly coated. Serve immediately, sprinkled with chopped parsley.

Hot Tomato and Mozzarella Salad

A quick, easy appetizer with a Mediterranean flavor. It can be prepared in advance, chilled, then broiled just before serving.

INGREDIENTS

Serves 4

1lb plum tomatoes, sliced
8oz mozzarella cheese, sliced
1 red onion, finely chopped
4–6 pieces sun-dried tomatoes in oil, drained and chopped
4 tbsp olive oil
1 tsp red wine vinegar
½ tsp Dijon mustard
4 tbsp chopped fresh mixed herbs, such as basil, parsley, oregano and chives
salt and black pepper
fresh herb sprigs, to garnish (optional)

1 Arrange the sliced tomatoes and mozzarella in circles in four individual shallow flameproof dishes.

2 Scatter over the chopped onion and sun-dried tomatoes.

3 Whisk together the olive oil, vinegar, mustard, chopped herbs and seasoning. Pour over the salads.

4 Place the salads under a hot broiler for 4–5 minutes, until the mozzarella starts to melt. Grind over plenty of black pepper and serve garnished with fresh herb sprigs, if liked.

Asparagus with Tarragon Butter

Eating fresh asparagus with your fingers can be messy, but it is the only proper way to eat it!

INGREDIENTS

Serves 4

1¼lb fresh asparagus
½ cup butter
2 tbsp chopped fresh tarragon
1 tbsp chopped fresh parsley
grated rind of ½ lemon
1 tbsp lemon juice
salt and black pepper

------ COOK'S TIP ------
When buying fresh asparagus, choose spears which are plump and have a good even color with tightly budded tips.

1 Trim the woody ends from the asparagus spears, then tie them into four equal bundles.

2 Place the bundles of asparagus in a large frying pan with about 1in boiling water. Cover and cook for about 6–8 minutes, until the asparagus is tender but still firm. Drain well and discard the strings.

3 Meanwhile, melt the butter in a small pan. Add the tarragon, parsley, lemon rind and juice and seasoning.

4 Arrange the asparagus spears on four warmed serving plates. Pour the hot tarragon butter over the asparagus and serve at once.

INDEX